Teach'n Beginning Offensive Basketball Drills, Plays, and Games Free Flow Handbook

By
Bob Swope

Series 5, Vol. 11 Free Flow Paperback Edition
Copyright 2013 Bob Swope
ISBN 13: 9780991115105

TABLE OF CONTENTS

1. Warning

If your kids, players on your team, or the participants have any physically limiting conditions, bleeding disorder, high blood pressure, any kind of heart condition, pregnancy or any other condition that may limit them physically, you should have them check with their doctor before letting them participate in any of the drills, plays, games, activities, or exercises discussed in this book.

Be sure participants in these drills, plays, games, or exercises that might make hard contact with any of the other participants are all approximately of the same weight and size to avoid a possible injury.

All of the drills, plays, exercises, and games for kids discussed in this book should be supervised by a competent adult, coach, or a professional using all the required equipment and safety procedures. **AUTHOR ASSUMES NO LIABILITY FOR ANY ACCIDENTAL INJURY OR EVEN DEATH THAT MAY RESULT FROM USING ANY OF THE BASKETBALL TECHNIQUES DISCUSSED IN THS BOOK.**

Extra care and caution should be taken with any of the drills in this book where players may accidentally get hit with any thrown or passed basketballs while using the drills discussed in this book. Especially where a hard thrown ball is coming right at the player because they may be the more dangerous things to watch for. Also watch for over exertion (heat stroke and heart problems) to any of your kids or players on a hot court or a hot day, Having a "defibrillator" near by would be a big help in case something happens.

Bob Swope
Jacobob Press LLC
Publisher

2. Introduction

My Interest and Intent

Occasionally youth basketball coaches have asked me about basic Offensive drills, plays, strategies, tactics and games that would be good to have all in one book, to use for training purposes. This handbook is intended to be a supplemental book to my "Teach'n Basketball" book. It is orientated more for the beginner basketball coach, rather than parents at home teaching fundamentals. However, parents can help their kids by getting them to work on the drills, plays, tactics, and strategies in this book. We will break this down into where your players are in their training, and what they are doing at that stage of their training. Also what drills, strategies, plays and tactics to use that will accomplish your goals in teaching them. My suggestion is use the time you have each week to maximize what you want to teach. For the younger 6 -11 years of age kids it's better to break practice drills down into more than one small group to keep everyone busy so that they don't get bored. This is not always easy to do because many coaches only want things done their way, and they don't always trust a helper assistant to do it their way. However, sooner or later you need to trust assistants to help get more done. It's in the best interest of the kids.

3. Discussion

Training Sessions

Some of the beginning basketball practices I've seen will only last about an hour and 30 minutes. This is where one coach has the whole group. I have seen coaches spending 15 to 20 minutes warming up and stretching. That leaves only 70 or so minutes to instruct, not counting the water breaks. And it's not-always one-on one instruction. This means you need to manage your time efficiently. You should limit the warm-up and stretching, so you can utilize the whole practice time. The other thing that is important is how many times a week is your practice. If it's only one day a week, you better sit down and make a schedule, so you can cover all the things they need to learn. Then follow it. If you have more time, like two hours, you can teach even more fundamentals.

Time

Generally keep your training time to around 15 minutes per drill being explained, especially if you have a group unless otherwise noted. Now here is where your training techniques may need to change. If you have a helper you can split into two groups. As an example, you might be teaching "shooting" and your assistant "dribbling." Then after 15 minutes you switch or rotate groups. This is because traditionally there is a lot of techniques to teach to beginning kids. In other words always keep your kids busy doing something at all times except for water breaks. Don't have any kids just standing around waiting because there is only one coach. You don't get as much teaching in that way, within any one practice. Also young kids traditionally get bored easily if you don't keep them busy for the entire training session.

Session Suggestions

I suggest getting as many assistant coaches as you can, then explain to them individually what they are responsible for teaching at their station. Tell your staff to learn all the kids names the first day if possible. Time wise plan your whole practice session. The kids will learn more in the short periods of time you have for teaching each day or week. As for the teaching methods we suggest using the "IDEA" slogan approach. Introduce, Demonstrate, Explain what you are teaching, and Attend to all the players in the group.

The Opponent

If it's possible, it could be beneficial to understand what tendencies your opponent has. Your players need to learn how to quickly figure out what their opponent is doing against them defensively. Your players should recognize the importance of this strategy, especially after playing an opponent more than once. Here is a little strategy you can employ as their coach. Keep a small pad of paper in your pocket and take notes. Look for weaknesses, then when it's game time, you can pick the offensive strategies that will attack, counterattack, and defeat what the opponent is doing. Start teaching your young players to have a game plan before they go into a game, then test them to make sure and remember what it is. Also have a back up plans in case your first plan didn't work and you need to change plans and tactics.

Pre Practice/Game Warm Up

Before your team starts to practice or get in a game, they need to go through a little warm up to get their muscles warmed up and stretched out. We will give you a nice little quick warm up routine to use. 10 minutes should do it. Once your kids learn it, they can do it on their own as a group. If you can teach them to do this well, and look good at it, your opponent may be impressed or intimidated by your teams discipline and focus. The organized warm up may put you at an advantage, as your opponent's may be a little psyched out.

Drills

I am going to refer to the drills as "Skill Training Activities" because that's what they really are. Also I am going to throw in a newer term now being used a lot. It is called "Core Training". What it does is train their body to make certain moves that will make them a better player. Drills will be organized by *"numbers"* so that your assistant coaches can use them and become more familiar with them that way. This way you are all on the same page as they say.

Techniques

For easy reference the techniques will be organized by *"numbers"* also. They will be arranged in the different offensive techniques and tactics. Each technique or tactic will have a short explanation for how it is supposed to work, strong points, what it is designed to accomplish.

Game Type Scrimmages

It's a good idea to introduce game type scrimmages once in a while. Beginners sometimes have a tendency to get bored with constant drilling. They want to see what it's like to go out and play in a game against an actual opponent. You need to referee these games just like in a real game. Just don't get frustrated by expecting perfect play by beginners. Have several spotters, each watching some particular aspect of their offensive play. As they get better you can be more particular about calling scores and penalties.

Core Training Games

Many coaches over the years have asked me to give them some "core training" games they can have the kids play once in a while at practices. Not just any games though, but games that will help develop their "core training" and "muscle memory" in a particular skill. So we are adding some games that will do just that. For easy reference these games will be organized by *"numbers"* also. Some of the time it's hard for coaches to buy into these games, but the more you play them, the more you will see your player's agility, speed and skills improving. Each game will have a short explanation for how it is supposed to work, strong points, and what the game is designed to accomplish.

4. Strategies and Tactics

The first strategy I recommend is "have a game plan" to match your team with their opponent. Try to watch their opponent warming up, and make some notes. Remember though these are only kids, so coach accordingly with your strategies and tactics if you are working with kids 7-11 years of age. You know the old "KISS" (Keep-It-Simple-Stupid) phrase. In advanced levels of basketball the players have special offensive roles to play. However, for beginners it's important to teach them that everyone on the field plays offense and defense. Here are just a few very basic strategies and some tactics you can use for young beginning teams that should prove to be helpful.

Offense

Basic Team Strategies and Concepts
1. If you have a team of young players that are not too good with their offensive techniques or skills have them all work on their weakest skill or skills at home around the garage basket every chance they get.
2. Teach your players that offense is also based on a teamwork concept, not just a lot of individual star players shooting baskets.
3. Figure out if your opponents are using a "possession style" or "fast break style" of offense, then coach your team accordingly.

4. The minute your team loses offensive possession of the ball teach them to transition quickly and be ready to defend the "space" through and behind their defense.

5. If you have a big tall center, and the other team does not, then put your center near the basket in the lo- post, and get the ball to them. Teach them to jump _way up_ when they shoot, they may make the basket, and draw some fouls that way.

6. If you have one of the faster teams in your division, then use a fast break, or a motion offense.

7. If your team is good at ball handling, then you can use just about any of the offenses, depending on who you are playing, and what their strengths are.

Individual Strategies and Concepts

1. Tell your players to not try to do too much, just learn and do their job.

2. Teach your players to always look for an open player down the court, don't try to dribble the ball all the way to the basket every time they get it.

3. When they are sitting on the bench or in position waiting for the play to come to them, tell them to be alert at noticing what the player guarding them is doing. Look for a weakness.

4. Tell them to learn how to become the best ball handler they can be.

Beginners Simple Offensive Role Playing Strategies

1. Each player has a role to play and a position on the court to maintain. Once you have assigned your players to a position have them learn the role they play at that position.

2. Guards are out in front. Their basic job is get the inbounds pass then get the ball down the court quickly and set up plays. They are usually smaller and faster.

3. Forwards move down the court usually to the outside or around the edge of the key. They are usually bigger and taller and good jump shot shooters. Their role is usually try to get in an open position to take a shot.

4. Centers are usually right around or under the basket. But sometimes they play a high post at the top of the key. Their role is get passes around the basket then out jump opponents and make baskets. Their role is also to grab the rebounds away from opponents. They are usually one of the tallest players on the team.

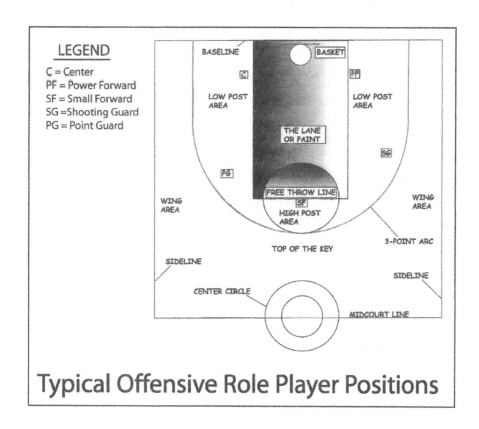

Typical Offensive Role Player Positions

Other Tactics and Styles of Play

There are other styles of play for offense. What style you play will depend on you and what style you are comfortable with it as a coach. However, you should know about some of these because if you have the right players it could make your team or players better. These styles do vary quite a bit all over the world though. It will come down to what your players are capable of.

Basic Offensive Styles

1. Simple Basic Offense
2. Zone Offenses
3. Motion Offenses
4. Transition Offenses
5. Out of Bounds Offenses
6. Breaking the Press Offenses
7. Delay Offenses
8. Tip Off Offenses

Further along in the book we will give the different plays you can run in each one of these different styles. And we will explain how they work.

5. Warm Up Exercises

I'm going to give you a quick warm up routine you can use to get your kids warmed up and their muscles stretched. Teach your players how to do these group exercises all by themselves. Here is an idea I have used before. When you are warming up your team, you can try this. Have your captain or a respected teammate stand in front of the group, and lead the routine. Teach your players to count slowly and out loud. The team alternates counting, when the leaders yell. "One," the group yells, "Two," etc. You only need to do six reps of each exercise. It's really a "psyche out" for any opponent's watching. And you may need this edge if the opponent's are more experienced or stronger players. You are only looking at about 10 minutes to go through these.

The Simple Routine

1. Start by doing 10 jumping jacks to get their muscles warmed up.
2. Next slowly do 6 "seated hamstring/quadriceps stretches.
3. Next slowly do 3 pelvic stretches on each side, holding for 3 seconds between them.
4. Next slowly do 6 push forward pull back ankle stretches.
5. Next slowly do 3 front quadriceps stretches on both thighs, leaning forward and holding for 3 seconds between them.
6. Next slowly do 6 rear shoulder stretches, holding for 3 seconds.
7. Next slowly do 3 front shoulder stretches on each shoulder, holding for 3 seconds between them.
8. Last use a teammate, or find a wall, and slowly do 3 calf stretches on each leg, holding it 3 seconds between them.

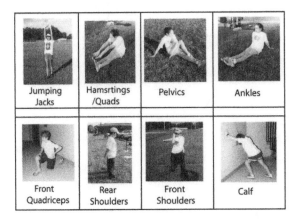

6. Offensive Skill Training Activities

Note: ALL ACTIVITIES will be numbered for "EASY" reference.

The offensive drills will cover all the types of skills that young kids learning to play offensive basketball need to know to get started off on the right foot. Some are "Core Training" and most all involve "Muscle Memory" training. They train the body, arms, legs and feet of your players to make certain moves and decisions that will make them a better player. Offensive players have to be poised, and patient. The guards see the whole court and they talk to their teammates. Basically they try to move he ball down the court and attempt to make baskets, or set up teammates to shoot them.

The skill activities are numbered so that you can have your assistant coach(s) use them and become more familiar with them for reference purposes. These skill activities will cover the very basic fundaments like shooting, passing, dribbling, ball handling. We will also try to cover some of the little special techniques that will help them. The plan is stay with small training groups, where you or one of your coaches is teaching one of these skills. Keep the time period short, maybe 15 minutes on the group to group activities. Then blow a whistle and one group moves over to the next group.

The size of your groups will depend on how many kids you have in your training session, and how many instructors (coaches) you have. As an example if you have 12 kids on your team, then you could have 2 groups of 6. Then you would need 2 stations and at least one instructor or coach per group. The bigger your group is though the more problems you will have. Smaller groups mean more touches, and more teaching control on your part. However, some drills may need to be combined for bigger groups in order to teach similar techniques more smoothly and quicker. If you can find them, have an instructor and an assistant at each station, then show them what to do. Most coaches don't like to do this even if they may need to because of a large group size, but using parents as assistants and showing them exactly what you want them to do can work. I do this all the time and it works great for me with young kids. Parents are usually just sitting around watching with nothing to do anyway, so why not get them involved and put them to work. You would be surprised at how many parents are willing to help, not a lot but quite a few. And that's all you need. Just show them *EXACTLY* what you want them to do

Here is another technique that works great with young kids. They have a short attention span. So when you need to just talk to all of them, then make them sit down cross legged, Indian style, or take a knee, and in a semi circle around in front of you. When you do it this way, they have less of a tendency to mess around, especially with boys, who talk too much when you are talking . Don't let them stand up, that's when the listening usually tends to stop and distractions set in.

Additional Help for Activities

If you are a beginning coach, and you are having trouble understanding how to implement these offensive activities in more detail, get a copy of "Teach'n Basketball" book. This is our teaching book for basketball, and it goes into more detail on exactly how to teach kids the particular skill we are discussing.

Legend for All Diagrams
(Unless otherwise spelled out in the diagram or section)

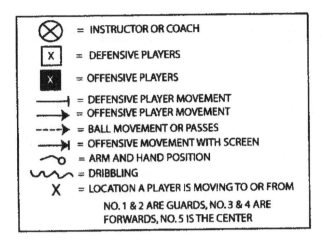

⊗	= INSTRUCTOR OR COACH
X (white box)	= DEFENSIVE PLAYERS
X (black box)	= OFFENSIVE PLAYERS
⊢——	= DEFENSIVE PLAYER MOVEMENT
——▶	= OFFENSIVE PLAYER MOVEMENT
----▶	= BALL MOVEMENT OR PASSES
——▶I	= OFFENSIVE MOVEMENT WITH SCREEN
∿o	= ARM AND HAND POSITION
∿∿	= DRIBBLING
X	= LOCATION A PLAYER IS MOVING TO OR FROM

NO. 1 & 2 ARE GUARDS, NO. 3 & 4 ARE
FORWARDS, NO. 5 IS THE CENTER

Basic Offensive Skills

SHOOTING DRILLS AND SKILLS

The Bank Shot (No.1)

Object of the activity: Teach all your players how to make the close in bank shots.

What you will need: You will need a regulation height basket, a basketball and one or two coaches, and a whistle.

Working the activity: One player (P1) stands off the left of the basket, the other players line up out to the right of the basket just outside of the 3 point circle. P1 starts with the ball and either bounce passes it or straight passes it to P2 who dribbles to the basket for a lay up. What they have to do though is bank the ball in every time off the backboard square. Basically they aim for the center of the square *PAINTED ON THE* backboard. In time they will see that they have to adjust that a little. P1 waits, rebounds, and passes to the next player in the line. Then P1 goes to the end of the line and P2 becomes the new P1. Run the drill fast. At the lower levels this is the most *important* drill to work on for "core memory".

Emphasize: aiming, focusing, and hitting the center of the blackboard square.

Run this activity: for about 15 minutes and making sure each player gets at least 5 attempts at shooting at the basket. If players are not catching on have an assistant coach pull them aside and show them what they are doing wrong so that the practice does not stop and keeps going.

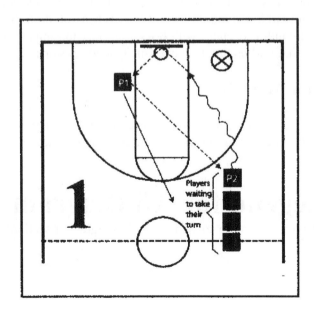

The Baby Jumper Shot (No.2)

Object of the activity: Teach all your players how to make the close in baby jumper shots.

What you will need: You will need a regulation height basket, a basketball, one or two coaches, and a whistle.

Working the activity: The first player in the line passes the ball to P2, who stands with their back to the basket. The pass can be bounce, lob, or straight. P2 whirls around and takes a jump shot into the basket. P1 rebounds. The next player in line moves to P2. While this is happening P1 passes to the next player at the front of the line, then moves to the end of the line. P2 moves to the P1 position after shooting, and the old P1 moves to the end of the line. Then the whole process starts over again with the front player in the line passing to P2. Make sure P2 gets way up in the air on their jump shot. Run the drill fast.

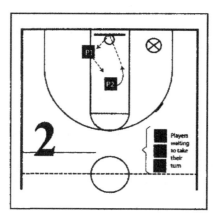

Emphasize: jumping high up in the air to make a set type jump shot.

Run this activity: for about 15 minutes and making sure each player gets at least 5 attempts at shooting at the basket. If players are not catching on have an assistant coach pull them aside and show them what they are doing wrong so that the practice does not stop and keeps going.

Beginners Lay on the Floor Training (No.3)

Object of the activity: Teach all your players the correct wrist and hand action for shooting a basketball.

What you will need: You will need a floor, some up in the air vertical room, a basketball, one or two coaches, and a whistle.

Working the activity: This is a real simple lay on the floor on their back, push the ball straight up, catch it with only one hand, and push it back up again skill activity. If there are 5 in the group they can all lay on their backs in a circle, heads to the outside, with the coach in the middle observing. Have them push the ball straight up, then catch it with the same hand without dropping it. Have them do this at least 5 times with each hand. Rest a minute or so then do another 5 pushes with each hand.

Emphasize: the wrist action (goose neck) of the shooting hand and the support of the off hand for control.

Run this activity: for about 15 minutes and making sure each player gets at least 5 attempts at shooting the ball up in the air while lying on their back. If players are not catching on have an assistant coach pull them aside and show them what they are doing wrong so that the practice does not stop and keeps going.

Beginners Sit on the Chair Training (No.4)

Object of the activity: Teach all your players the correct wrist and hand action for shooting the set shot. This drill is also for building up arm strength to get the ball to the basket.

What you will need: You will need a floor, some clear room around a basket, a basketball, one or two coaches, and a whistle. One coach to instruct and one coach to return the shoots at the basket.

Working the activity: This is a real simple. Set up some gym folding chairs spread at 3 places around the basket. The distance from the basket will depend on the size of the players. You could start at 10 or 12 feet away from the basket for the real little kids and move out from there. The rule is start from close enough for the players shot to reach the basket. Their shot should be a one hand with support set shot. After they get better and their arm strength is good you can get rid of the chair. Have players line up behind each chair and take turns. Each player gets 3 straight shots then goes to the end of another line behind a chair. A coach collects their shots and returns the ball to them. Another alternative is have 3 of the players not shooting collect and return the balls.

Emphasize: the wrist action of the shooting hand, support of the off hand for control, and push off strength.

Run this activity: for about 15 minutes and making sure each player gets at least 5 attempts at shooting the ball up in the air while lying on their back. If players are not catching on have an assistant coach pull them aside and show them what they are doing wrong so that the practice does not stop and keeps going.

Around the Chair Screen Drill (No.5)

Object of the activity: Teach all your players how to move around a simulated screen and take the shot.

What you will need: You will need a floor, some clear room around a basket, a basketball, one or two coaches, and a whistle. One coach to instruct and one coach to return the shoots at the basket. Or you can use the extra kids to return the shots to the next shooter, but don't forget to rotate them. This keeps the drill moving

Working the activity: This is a real simple. Set up a gym folding chair at the foul shot line. Have the players line up in back. The first player steps up just to the left of the top of the key. Coach feed them a pass, they take the pass, dribble around the chair and take a short jump set shot at the basket. Player then goes to the end of the line. The ball is returned to the next shooter.

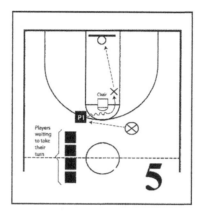

Emphasize; player dribbling quickly around the chair (the simulated screen) then popping up high for the jump set shot.

Run this activity: for about 15 minutes and making sure each player gets at least 5 attempts at shooting the jump shot. If players are not catching on have an assistant coach pull them aside and show them what they are doing wrong so that the practice does not stop and keeps going.

Holding the Ball Training (No.6)

Object of the activity: Teach all your players the correct way to hold and stabilize the ball for a shot.

What you will need: You will need a little room on the court, or some room around a garage basket, a basketball, one or two coaches, and a whistle. One coach to instruct and one coach to pass players the ball.

Working the activity: This is a real simple. The very first thing to teach players is how to hold the ball. The second thing to explain to them is, control the ball with their finger tips. There is more than one way to hold the ball, but there is one way that is more effective, especially for the younger kids. First have them put the ball in the palm of their strong hand (usually the right). It should rest on the pads of the hand between the thumb and the fingers, and with some space between the palm and the ball. Then support, and steady, the ball with the other hand ***(SEE FIGURE 6)***. Next have them grip the seams, with the fingertips of the pushing hand. The fingers that propel the ball are the "index", and "middle", fingers. These two fingers should be in the center of the ball. Coaches have found a good way to accomplish this. And that is have them place these two fingers around the valve. Have them stand out in front of you about 6 feet away. Then take the ball and pass or toss it to them. What they have to do is catch it, spin the ball around, with the non shooting hand until the valve is centered in the fingers. Once they have done that, they just pass the ball back to you and go to the end of the line. Keep doing this, over and over until they get in the habit of doing this automatically.

Emphasize: getting their fingers correctly across the seams of the ball.

Run this activity: for about 15 minutes and making sure each player gets at least 5 attempts at properly holding the ball with each hand. If players are not catching on have an assistant coach pull them aside and show them what they are doing wrong so that the practice does not stop and keeps going.

Proper Shooting Stance Training (No.7)

Object of the activity: Teach all your players the correct stance when they are ready to shoot the ball.

What you will need: You will need a little room on the court out near the free throw line, or about the same room around a garage basket, a basketball, one coach to instruct, and a whistle.

Working the activity: This is a real simple. The very first thing to teach players is how to hold the ball and position it in their hands. Basically they hold the ball the same way as in Training No.6. Have the rest of the players line up behind the player doing the training. Have the player just casually hold the ball. Then when your players get ready to shoot the ball, they should have their feet and shoulders squared up (Facing) to the basket. Sometimes in the game it's hard to get squared up to the basket so have them do the best they can. When practicing though they should always try to do this. The foot, on the side of the shooting hand , should be just a little bit out in front of the other foot. The ball should be held just above, or below the knee, for the 5 and 6 year olds. It can be up higher, around the waist or chest, for the bigger kids. It kind of depends on the arm strength the shooter has ***(SEE FIGURE.7)***. For left handed shooters this stance is going to be flip flopped or just the opposite. All players need to work on this drill. Players should learn to get into this stance right and left handed.

Have the player take the ball, and go out to the free throw line. Have them relax. Then blow the whistle and have them get into the stance correctly. Stand under the basket, watch them, and check their form. Make any necessary corrections. Have them stand there and just relax again. Then blow the whistle and have them get into the stance again. Keep doing this over and over until they get in the habit of doing this automatically. After going through this several times have them work on it with the opposite hand. Keep doing this with them, over and over until they get in the habit of doing this automatically.

Emphasize; squaring up and facing the direction they are going to shoot in

Run this activity: for about 15 minutes and making sure each player gets at least 2 attempts with both their right and left hand. If players are not catching on have an assistant coach pull them aside and show them what they are doing wrong so that the practice does not stop and keeps going.

Proper Body Mechanics for Shooting Training (No.8,9)

Object of the activity: Teach all your players the correct body mechanics for shooting which will give the ball a better chance at going in the basket.

What you will need: You will need a little room on the court out near the free throw line, or about the same room around a garage basket, a basketball, one coach to instruct, and a whistle.

Working the activity: This is a real simple. Tell them that their head should remain still, all the way through the shot until the ball goes in, or hits the basket. The eyes need to stay on the target. For a target, have them focus on the center of the square painted on the back board. The eyes should stay focused on the target, all the way through the shot until the ball goes in, or hits the basket. Tell them that their arm, and the ball, should not block their vision as they focus on the basket *(SEE FIGURE 8)*. They need to be positioned, so they can see the basket with both eyes. A little jump up on the shot is ok, but not forward. The body *should not* drift, or sway from side to side, or fall back during the shot. This will all throw off their balance, and cause the shot to be out of line with the basket. Less body motion during the shot will give you a better chance of making it. The back foot, on the side opposite the shooting hand, should be turned outward *(SEE FIGURE 9)*.

Have the player take the ball, and go out to the free throw line. Have them relax. Then blow the whistle and have them get into the stance correctly. Stand under the basket, watch them, and check their form. Make any necessary corrections. Have them stand there and just relax again. Then blow the whistle, and have them get into the stance again. Keep doing this over and over until they get in the habit of doing this automatically. After going through this several times have them work on it with their head to the opposite side. Keep doing this with them, over and over until they get in the habit of doing this automatically. You can have them shoot at the basket if you like.

Right **8** Wrong

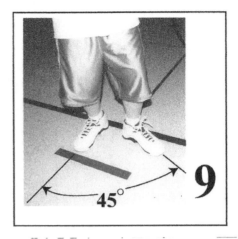

45° **9**

Emphasize; not blocking their view of the basket with the ball.

Run this activity: for about 15 minutes and making sure each player gets at least 2 attempts with both their right and left hand. If players are not catching on have an assistant coach pull them aside and show them what they are doing wrong so that the practice does not stop and keeps going. If the little kids don't get it they can try again another time.

Proper Shooting Mechanics Training (No.10,11,12)

Object of the activity: Teach all your players the correct shooting mechanics which will give the ball a better chance at going in the basket.

What you will need: You will need a little room on the court out near the free throw line, or about the same room around a garage basket, a basketball, one coach to instruct, and a whistle.

Working the activity: This is a real simple. Tell them that their head should remain still, all the way through the shot until the ball goes in, or hits the basket. The eyes need to stay on the target. For a target, have them focus on the center of the square painted on the back board. The eyes should stay focused on the target, all the way through the shot until the ball goes in, or hits the basket. Tell them that their arm, and the ball, should not block their vision as they focus on the basket *(SEE FIGURE 8)*. They need to be positioned, so they can see the basket with both eyes. A little jump up on the shot is ok, but only straight up not forward. The body _should not_ drift, or sway from side to side, or fall back during the shot *(SEE FIGURE 10)*. This will all throw off their balance, and cause the shot to be out of line with the basket. Less body motion during the shot will give them a better chance of making it. The back foot, on the side opposite the shooting hand, should be pointed at 45 degrees outward on *free throws*, to help the player stay in balance better when starting the shot *(SEE FIGURE 9)*. But this is only on free throws. It won't work on moving shots. On moving shots, they should land in the same place with their feet that they jumped from, or maybe just a little bit forward of that spot. All players need to work on this drill. Have them go back to the free throw line as in the previous drill. Then a coach gets under the basket and watch their form. Blow a whistle," and have them get into the shooting stance *(SEE FIGURE 7)*. Next have them slowly take a jump shot *(SEE FIGURE 11)* and check all of their body mechanics as they make the shot. Make any necessary corrections, and have them keep executing shots. Practice makes perfect.

Practice these techniques the same way as in "Training 8, 9, except stand first directly behind them, and then in front of them, to make sure you can see that they are following the shooting and body mechanics correctly. On free throw shots, make sure they are keeping the back foot turned outward *(SEE FIGURE 9)*. Also make sure they stay balanced while shooting. First have them make some free throw shots. After they have tried some free throw shots, have them dribble up to the free throw line and make some jump shots. What they have to do in this case is, dribble really low, scoop the ball up by rolling the shooting hand around underneath, and explode into the "jump up set shot" *(SEE FIGURE 11)*. Next they push up hard, set the ball with their hands, and make the shot. Also see the Jump Shot, Drill No. 17.

C   B   A
10

11

12

Emphasize; getting their feet in the right position.

Run this activity: for about 15 minutes and making sure each player gets at least 2 attempts with both their right and left hand. If players are not catching on have an assistant coach pull them aside and show them what they are doing wrong so that the practice does not stop and keeps going. If the little kids don't get it right away they can try again another time.

Release, Follow Through, and Arc Shooting Training (No.13, 14, 15)

Object of the activity: Teach all your players the correct mechanics and follow through for shooting which will give the ball a better chance at going in the basket.

What you will need: You will need a little room on the court out near the free throw line, or about the same room around a garage basket, a basketball, one coach to instruct, and a whistle. Also the little kids can use No. 3 and 4 training drills to help their mechanics.

Working the activity: This is a real simple. The release, follow through, and arc, on the ball are very important, in finishing the shot. For the release, the ball should be placed just above the eye on the shooting hand side, and moved just to the outside enough to still be able to see the basket *(SEE FIGURE 8)*. The elbow on the shooting hand needs to pointed at, and aligned with the basket *(SEE FIGURE 13)*. The wrist should snap forward, with the "index", and "middle", finger rolling off the ball, and causing it to back spin a lot. These two fingers should be the last to touch the ball as it rolls off, and that is where the good spin is generated. The push has to be upward, and not forward. On the follow through, after the ball has been released, the wrist is bent over forward forming what has been called "a gooseneck" *(SEE FIGURE 14)*. Also on the follow

15

through, keep your eyes focused on the target all the way to the basket. Another little aid to the shot is, imagine you are grabbing the front rim with the shooting hand, just after you release the ball. To get just the right arc on the shot, sometimes takes lots of trial and error evaluation. Too hard a push, and too much arc, and the ball will hit way up on the back board. Too little arc, and the ball may fall short of the basket. All players need to work on this drill.

Some coaches have come up with a way to check if your release and follow through are correct, or if they have flaws. What they do is take a 3/4 or 1 inch wide strip of white tape, wrap it around the center of the basketball, and perpendicular to the seams *(SEE FIGURE 15)*. Then they have the player stand at the free throw line and make a jump shot. By standing behind them, you look to see if the ball appears to be wobbling as goes up to the basket. If it does appear to be wobbling, then the player has a flaw in their release, follow through, or grip. If the ball is rotating symmetrically it will not appear to be wobbling, and their technique is ok.

Emphasize; Getting the best and straightest trajectory to the basket without the ball wobbling.
Run this activity: for about 15 minutes and making sure each player gets at least 2 attempts at shooting with both their right and left hand. If players are not catching on have an assistant coach pull them aside and show them what they are doing wrong so that the practice does not stop and keeps going. If the little kids don't get it right away they can try again another time.

7. TYPES OF SHOTS

Note: The different types of shots will be numbered for "EASY " reference.

We will try to cover all the basic types of shots that young kids learning to play offensive basketball need to know to get started off on the right foot. Some are "Core Training" and most all involve "Muscle Memory" training. They train the body, arms, legs and feet of your players to Use the correct mechanics to make the shot.

Teaching Techniques
The shots are numbered so that you can have your assistant coach(s) use them and become more familiar with them for reference purposes. These skill activities will cover the very basic fundaments. We will also try to cover some of the little special techniques that will help them make the shots. The plan is stay with small training groups, where you or one of your coaches is teaching one of these shots at another basket. Some gyms will have as many as 6 separate baskets to use. With enough assistants or parents helping, you could be teaching 4 different shots in an hours time by rotating basket to basket. Keep the time period short, maybe 10 to 15 minutes on the group to group activities. Then blow a whistle and each group moves over to the next basket.

The size of your groups will depend on how many kids you have in your training session, and how many instructors (coaches) you have. As an example if you have 16 kids on your team, then you could have 4 groups of 4, each learning a different shot. You will probably need at least 4 assistants or parents helping to pull off this type of training though. The bigger your group is though the more problems you will have. Smaller groups mean more touches, and more teaching control on your part. However, some drills may need to be combined for bigger groups in order to teach similar combination player techniques more smoothly and quicker. If you can find them, have an instructor and an assistant at each station, then show them exactly what you want them to do.

Many coaches don't like to do this even if they may need to because of a large group size, but using parents as assistants and showing them exactly what you want them to do can work. I do this all the time and it works great for me with young kids. Parents are usually just sitting around watching with nothing to do anyway, so why not get them involved and put them to work. You would be surprised at how many parents are willing to help, not a lot but quite a few. And that's all you need. The trick is just show them *EXACTLY* what you want them to do

Lay Up Shot Training (No.16)
Object of the activity: Teach all your players the correct mechanics and follow through for shooting lay ups.
What you will need: You will need a little room on the court around the basket, a basketball and possibly a whistle.
The Basics Are: This is a shot where a player generally breaks away and comes into the basket at a high rate of speed, leaps up and kind of scoop finger rolls the ball into the basket. It's called a "lay up" because with a lot of momentum and one arm extended you kind of lay the ball up towards the backboard and into the basket. The secret is the underhanded scoop approach. This way if a defender is right behind them they would need to go over the top of them (possible foul) to reach and block the shot. Where if you bring the ball back to your shoulder to push it up like a jumper it makes it easier to block from behind.
Working the activity: Give the players a ball and have them line up back out by the 3-point circle line. To get more shots in have players alternate, one coming in from the right side and then .one coming in from the left side. You will need a ball shagger to collect and quickly return the bolls to the shooters.

Emphasize; the finger roll and arm extension towards the center of the backboard square

Run this activity: for about 10 to 15 minutes and making sure each player gets at least 2 attempts at shooting while coming in from both the right and left side of the basket. If players are not catching on have an assistant coach pull them aside and show them what they are doing wrong so that the practice does not stop and keeps going. If the little kids don't get it right away they can try again another time.

Set Shot Jumper Training (No.17)

Object of the activity: Teach all your players the correct mechanics and follow through for shooting set shot jumpers.

What you will need: You will need a little room on the court around the basket, a basketball, an acting defender, one coach, and possibly a whistle.

The Basics Are: This is a shot that can take many forms and styles. The baby jumper is in closer to the basket where the shooter is blocked from making a clear lay up. So they just pull up short when blocked, pop straight up and make a set shot jumper. Usually a defender will get in front of them and expect a player to attempt to charge through them to the basket so the defender stops, and sometimes leans waiting for the shooter to charge into them for a foul. So by stopping and popping up high they have a good chance of making the basket. Bigger players look to get free of defenders in front and close to them and then try for a long jumper or a 3-point shot.

Working the activity: Give the players a ball and have them line back out by the 3-point circle line. Younger players can be in closer. To get more shots in have players alternate, one coming in from the right side and then one coming in from the left side. Put the defender about 6 feet in front of them to block their path to the basket. Tell the defender not to attack, but just block their path forcing them to stop short and make a baby jumper. You will need a ball shagger to collect and quickly return the balls to the shooters.

Emphasize; stopping short then pushing or popping straight up for the set sot jumper

Run this activity: for about 10 to 15 minutes and making sure each player gets at least 2 attempts at shooting while coming in from both the right and left side of the basket to make their jumpers. If players are not catching on have an assistant coach pull them aside and show them what they are doing wrong so that the practice does not stop and keeps going.

Hook Shot Training (No.18)

Object of the activity: Teach all your players the correct mechanics and follow through for shooting hook shots.

What you will need: You will need a little room on the court around the basket, a basketball, an acting defender, one coach, and possibly a whistle.

The Basics Are: This is a shot that players can make in closer to the basket. The ideal technique is moving across from side to side and taking the shot over the top of the defenders head right in front of the basket. The arm is swung from the side with kind of a hooking effect over the top of the head *(SEE FIGURE 18-A)*. Players need to learn to make this shot with either hand. It will take more practice to make this shot with their non dominate side hand though.

Working the activity: Give the players a ball and have them line up back out about 6 or 8 feet away from the basket, first from the left side (right handers) then the right side (left handers). Put the defender about 5 feet in front of them to block their path to the basket. Tell the defender not to attack or block, but just slide across in front of them between them and the basket to simulate the blocker They jump up and make the shot when they dribble right in front of the basket. You will need a ball shagger to collect and quickly return the balls to the shooters.

C   B   A

18

Emphasize; the pushing off and jumping up off their non shooting hand side foot.

Run this activity: for about 10 to 15 minutes and making sure each player gets at least 2 attempts at shooting while coming in from both the right and left side of the basket to make their shots. If players are not catching on have an assistant coach pull them aside and show them what they are doing wrong so that the practice does not stop and keeps going.

Free Throw Shot Training (No.19)

Object of the activity: Teach all your players the correct mechanics and follow through for shooting free throw shots.

What you will need: You will need a little room on the court around the basket at the free throw line, a basketball, one coach, a ball shagger, and possibly a whistle.

The Basics Are: This is a shot that players need to learn how to make. The type of snot is a set shot like in a jump shot. It is a free shot after a foul which needs to go in the basket each time. Sometimes it's two free shots depending on the foul type. Another reason this is important is because you are getting this free shot because an opposing player has fouled you. And if the opposing player gets too many fouls, they are out of the game. To make a free throw, they have to stand 15 feet away from the basket on the free throw line. Both feet should be just back of the edge of the free throw line, and the front or lead foot should be right at the center of the line, pointed straight ahead *(SEE FIGURE 19-A)* . On the newer hard wood floors, there is a nail right on the center of the line. Start 5 through 8 year olds out about 6 to 10 feet away from the basket, and work their way back to 15 feet away as they get better. Have them take a deep breath and let it out slowly to make sure they are relaxed, and not nervous before they start the shot. Lets talk about the knees again here. The knees are what make this shot, its where your power up to the basket comes from. So, make sure they do the drills to make their legs strong. Again, have them imagine *Grabbing* the rim, right after they release the ball *(SEE FIGURE 19-B)*. All players need to work on this shot constantly, it's very important.

Working the activity: Give the players a ball at the free throw line. Check their feet and body position then on the whistle let them shoot. Make sure they make a goose neck with their shot hand and don't step over the free flow line on their follow through.

Emphasize; a little squat then pushing up with their shot and making the goose neck.

Run this activity: for about 10 to 15 minutes making sure each player gets at least 5 attempts at shooting a free throw. If players are not catching on have an assistant coach pull them aside and show them what they are doing wrong so that the practice does not stop and keeps going.

Tip In Shot Training (No.20)

Object of the activity: Teach all your players how to follow a regular shot in towards the basket and look for a "*TIP IN*" in case the shot does not go in.

What you will need: You will need a little room on the court around the basket at the free throw line, a basketball, one coach, a defender, a ball shagger, and possibly a whistle.

The Basics Are: This is a shot that players need to learn how to make. The type of shot is is just jumping up high and using the tips of the fingers to push a missed shot back up and into the basket before a defender grabs it or it hits the floor *(SEE FIGURE 20-B)*. All players need to work on this shot constantly, it's very important.

Working the activity: Give the players a ball at the free throw line. Have the defender stand right under the basket. The player makes a shot that misses the basket, then they follow their shot in towards the basket, jump up and try to tip the ball in over or away from the defender. Tell the defender that just for practice to let the player make the tip in, just kind of get in their way a little.

A **20** B

Emphasize; having them check where it appears the ball is going to come off the basket or backboard then go to the spot where it looks like it will come down and jump way up high to push tip the ball back into the basket.

Run this activity: for about 10 to 15 minutes making sure each player gets at least 5 attempts at shooting a "tip in.". If players are not catching on have an assistant coach pull them aside and show them what they are doing wrong so that the practice does not stop and keeps going.

Three Point Perimeter Shot Training (No.21)

Object of the activity: Teach all your players how to make three point perimeter shots. I'm not sure the younger kids are strong enough to make this shot, but you can try with them. If not then come back to it when they get a little older and stronger.

What you will need: You will need a little room on the court around the basket out at the three point circle, a basketball, one coach, a ball shagger, and possibly a whistle.

The Basics Are: This is a shot that the bigger older players need to learn how to make. This type of shot is just a jumper set shot *(SEE FIGURE 11).* from way out farther from the basket on the three point circle This shot will just take quite a lot of arm strength by young kids to get the ball up to the basket.

Working the activity: Give the players a ball out on the three point circle and let them shoot a jump set shot. If they are older and can't reach the basket with the shot they need to build up their arm strength using dumbbells.

Emphasize; getting enough arc on the trajectory to drop the ball into the basket. The best way to learn how to make this shot is just a lot of practice out at three point distance to judge the range.

Run this activity: for about 10 to 15 minutes making sure each player gets at least 5 attempts at shooting three point shots. If players are not catching on have an assistant coach pull them aside and show them what they are doing wrong so that the practice does not stop and keeps going.

8. PASSING THE BALL

Note: The different types of passes and drills will be numbered for "EASY " reference.

Passing the basketball is a very important phase of the basketball game. As many of the great coaches have said, "The quickest kid on the team can not outrun the ball." To get the ball up court quickly, or to get the ball to the open person, is what offensive basketball is about.. Passes are probably the most effective way to attack a defense, and get the ball up court. Before you start any passing drills with your players you might try this little demonstration just for fun. Tell them that anyone that can run from the baseline to mid court before you throw the ball to mid court , or from the garage out to the sidewalk, will get a free Hamburger, coke, and fries. To make it even more interesting, give them a three step head start before you throw the ball. Explain to them that this is why passing, to move the ball up court, is quicker than dribbling it up court. When ever they make a good pass make sure to make a big deal out of it, just like you would if they shoot a basket and score. Any player on the team, who can find the open person to get the ball to, is a very valuable player to the team. Impress on your players that when they make a good pass, they make it easier for their team mates to shoot the ball, and it demoralizes the opponents defense. Another good practice technique is have them practice after school by finding a wall and using it to get the ball back to them. This way they can get their passing practice in every day while its still light outside.

Teaching Techniques

The passes and drills are numbered so that you can have your assistant coach(s) use them and become more familiar with them for reference purposes. These skill activities will cover the very basic fundaments. We will also try to cover some of the little special techniques that will help them make the passes. The plan is stay with small training groups, where you or one of your coaches is teaching one of these passes or drills. Keep the time period short, maybe 10 to 15 minutes on the group to group activities. Then blow a whistle and each group moves over to the next group or station.

The size of your groups will depend on how many kids you have in your training session, and how many instructors (coaches) you have. As an example if you have 16 kids on your team, then you could have 4 groups of 4, each learning a different shot. You will probably need at least 4 assistants or parents helping to pull off this type of training. The bigger your group is though the more problems you will have. Smaller groups mean more touches, and more teaching control on your part. However, some drills may need to be combined for bigger groups in order to teach similar combination player techniques more smoothly and quicker. If you can find them, have an instructor and an assistant at each group or station, then show them exactly what you want them to do.

Many coaches don't like to do this, even if they may need to, because of a large group size, but using parents as assistants and showing them exactly what you want them to do can work. I do this all the time and it works great for me with young kids. Parents are usually just sitting around watching with nothing to do anyway, so why not get them involved and put them to work. You would be surprised at how many parents are willing to help, not a lot but quite a few. And that's all you need. The trick is just show them *EXACTLY* what you want them to do

Two Hands Chest Pass Training (No.22, 23)

Object of the activity: Teach all your players how to make a two hands chest pass.
What you will need: You will need a little room on the court, a wall, a basketball, one coach, and possibly a whistle.
The Basics Are: This is a pass that players need to learn how to make. It's the most common. This is push passing the ball in the air, using both hands. This drill is mostly for guards, and small forwards, but centers, and power forwards, also have to pass even though it's not as often. So, whatever position your players play, make sure to work at least a little bit each day with them on their passing skills. The basics for making a two handed pass are, have them grab the basketball with both hands and hold it at their chest level *(SEE FIGURE 22, STEP 1)*. Their thumbs should be facing in towards each other, just as they start the pass. As they are pushing out with the pass, their hands should be twisting to the outsides, with palms facing outward away from each other, thumbs down, just as they release the ball *(SEE FIGURE 22, STEP 2)*. Also they need to step out with the right foot if they are right handed, and the left foot if they are left handed *(SEE FIGURE 22)*. The stepping out helps them get more speed and power on the pass.

Working the activity: There are a number of ways to do this drill, but this way is one of the best. Give the players a ball and line them up in front of a wall about 15 feet away. The first player passes against the wall then goes to the end of the line. The next player in line catches the ball off the wall , makes their pass and goes to the end of the line. This just keeps repeating over and over. It teaches them to catch a pass them make a quick pass.

Alternative Way: This can also be accomplished by putting players in a big circle ***(SEE FIGURE 23)*** and having them pass the ball back and forth to another payer.

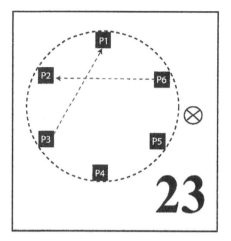

Emphasize; A good strong straight push right at the target.

Run this activity: for about 10 minutes making sure each player gets as many attempts as possible. If players are not catching on have an assistant coach pull them aside and show them what they are doing wrong so that the practice does not stop and keeps going.

Both Hands Bounce Pass Training (No.24)

Object of the activity: Teach all your players how to make a two hands bounce pass.

What you will need: You will need a little room on the court, a wall, a basketball, one coach, and possibly a whistle.

The Basics Are: This is a pass that players need to learn how to make. This is push passing the ball in a bounce to another player, using both hands. This drill is mostly for guards, and small forwards, but centers, and power forwards, also have to pass even though it's not as often. So, whatever position your players play, make sure to work at least a little bit each day with them on their passing skills. The basics for making a two handed bounce pass is, have them hold the ball in the same grip, and location as in the chest pass ***(SEE FIGURE 24, STEP 1)***. Except they push the ball hard, down against the floor or driveway. Starting out the pass is the same as the chest pass, however just as they release the ball, they rotate the palms outward, with their thumbs down. The hands should be facing outward, and slightly pointed downward on the follow through ***(SEE FIGURE 24, STEP 2)***. Also they need to learn how to aim the ball so that it hits the floor, or driveway, about three fourths of the way toward you. And it has to bounces back up into the receivers hands on one bounce. Also they need to step out with the left foot if they are left handed, and the right foot if they are right handed ***(SEE FIGURE 24)***. The stepping out helps them get more speed and power on the pass.

Working the activity: There are a number of ways to do this drill, but this way is one of the best. Give the players a ball and line them up in front of a wall about 15 feet away. The first player passes against the wall then goes to the end of the line. The next player in line catches the ball off the wall , makes their pass and goes to the end of the line. This just keeps repeating over and over. It teaches them to catch a pass them make a quick pass.

Alternative Way: This can also be accomplished by putting players in a big circle *(SEE FIGURE 23)* and having them pass the ball back and forth to another payer.

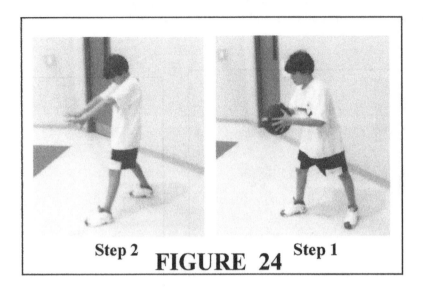

Step 2   **FIGURE 24**   Step 1

Emphasize; A good strong straight push bounce pass right at the target.

Run this activity: for about 10 minutes making sure each player gets as many attempts as possible. If players are not catching on have an assistant coach pull them aside and show them what they are doing wrong so that the practice does not stop and keeps going.

Two Hands Overhead Pass Training (No.25)

Object of the activity: Teach all your players how to make two handed overhead passes.

What you will need: You will need a little room on the court, a basketball, a wall, one coach, and possibly a whistle.

The Basics Are: This is a drill to work on one handed push passes. The basics for making the two handed overhead pass are, first have them grab the ball the same way as described in drill 22, except hold it up over the head *(SEE FIGURE 25, STEP 1)*. Then as they push and release the ball, out toward their target, they need to rotate the hands outward, thumbs down, and snap their wrists *(SEE FIGURE 25, STEP 2)*. If you don't snap your wrists the ball tends to sail high, and over the head of the person you want to get it to. Also they need to step way out with the foot on the strong hand side, to get more momentum and distance on the pass.

Working the activity: Work this just like the other pass training against the wall.

Emphasize; making a good strong overhead snap and release pass right at the target.

Run this activity: for about 10 minutes making sure each player gets as many attempts as possible. If players are not catching on have an assistant coach pull them aside and show them what they are doing wrong so that the practice does not stop and keeps going.

Step 2   FIGURE 25   Step 1

One Hand Pass Training (No.26, 27)

Object of the activity: Teach all your players how to make one handed passes.

What you will need: You will need a little room on the court, a basketball, a wall, one coach, and possibly a whistle.

The Basics Are: This is a drill to work on one handed push passes. The basics for making a one handed pass are, start out by grabbing it with both hands ***(SEE FIGURE 27, STEP 1)***. This is a must for little kids because their hands are so small. The weak hand supports the ball, and the strong hand is right behind the ball ***(SEE FIGURE 26)***. When you are ready to pass the ball, you step right at the player the pass is going to, using the left foot. Then you push it with your right hand, aiming the ball so it gets to the player about chest high ***(SEE FIGURE 27, STEP 2)***. One handed passes can be in the air, or bounced to a team mate. On the follow through the ball should roll off the finger tips.

Working the activity: Work this just like the other pass training against the wall.

Step 2   FIGURE 27   Step 1

FIGURE 26

Emphasize; making a good strong one handed straight push pass right at the target.

Run this activity: for about 10 minutes making sure each player gets as many attempts as possible. Have them alternate every other time first with the right then the left hand. If players are not catching on have an assistant coach pull them aside and show them what they are doing wrong so that the practice does not stop and keeps going.

Line Passing Drill (No.28)

Object of the activity: Teach all your players how to make all the passes.

What you will need: You will need a little room on the court, two basketballs, one coach, and possibly a whistle.

The Basics Are: This is a fast drill to work on all of the different types of passes. Chest passes, overhead passes, bounce passes , and one handed passes.

Working the activity: Have your players line up in 2 lines near center court and the free throw line facing each other about 12 to 15 feet apart. Each player has a basketball. Player P1 passes their ball to P2 then goes to the end of P2's line. P2 passes their ball to the next player behind P1, then goes to the end of P1's line. The player catching P2's ball passes their ball to the player behind P2, then goes to the end of P2's line and so on until player P1 and P2 get to the front of the lines again. Then they change the type of pass. Start out with everyone making a "chest" pass, then they all go to a "bounce" pass, then a "one handed" pass, and last an "overhead" pass. Some of the time have them fake to the right then to left before passing straight ahead.

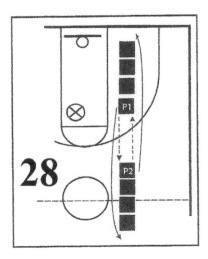

Emphasize; making a good strong straight push pass, whichever type, right at the target player.

Run this activity: for about 10 minutes making sure each player gets as many attempts as possible. If players are not catching on have an assistant coach pull them aside and show them what they are doing wrong so that the practice does not stop and keeps going.

Secondary Break Passing/ Shooting Drill (No.29)

Object of the activity: Teach all your players how to make passes to a moving player going to the basket..

What you will need: You will need a little room on the court, two lines of players, two basketballs, one coach, and possibly a whistle.

The Basics Are: This is a drill to work on the different types of passes to a moving player. Chest passes, bounce passes , and one handed passes.

Working the activity: Have your players break up into 2 half court groups. Have them get into 2 lines on each half court. One on the right wing, and one near the center circle. P1 takes the ball and dribbles towards the top of the key, stops, and passes to P2 on the right wing who has started to run towards the basket. P2 catches the pass, comes under control then takes a jump shot at the basket. Then they quickly follow their shot in, get the rebound, pass the ball back to the next player in line waiting at center court. Then they go to end of the P2 line. A new player takes the ball, dribbles up, and passes the ball to the next player in the P2 line who has started a run towards the basket. After one time through shooters go to the end of the dribbler/passer line. After one time through dribbler/passers go to the end of the shooting line. Then the process keeps going until each player has made at least 3 passes and shots. Then the shooting line moves over the left wing and the process starts again from the other side. Try to keep the lines small so that the drill keeps moving and the players get a lot of touches.

Emphasize; making a good strong straight push pass right at the moving target.

Run this activity: for about 15 to 20 minutes making sure each player gets as many attempts as possible. If players are not catching on have an assistant coach pull them aside and show them what they are doing wrong so that the practice does not stop and keeps going.

9. DRIBBLING THE BALL

Note: The dribbling training and drills will be numbered for "EASY " reference.

Dribbling the basketball is another very important part of the game of basketball. As a parent you should start teaching them how to dribble as soon as they are 5 years old. It is the number one and probably the hardest skill to learn in basketball. One good thing is, it won't cost too much to get them started, just a basketball and a hard surface is needed. It is a coordination skill, and if they keep working at it they can learn how to do it. Probably the first thing to explain to them about dribbling is, have them learn right from the start, to **use their fingertips and not the palm of the hand.** The fingertips is where the control comes from. And coaches here is a tip for you, the more they dribble the better they will get, and the better they get the more confidence they will have. Another tip, if you want to see how good they are doing then when you see they have been out practicing, then check their hands. The fingertips should be dirty and the palms clean.

They should learn also to **keep the bouncing ball close to them.** If you watch the good dribblers, the ball will be like a Yo-Yo on a string as they move around with it. The best way to start out practicing with them is, have them just stand still and get used to dribbling right in front of themselves, using the fingers. You need to supervise them closely at first, to make sure they are learning the concept correctly. Next you can have them walk slowly while dribbling. When they learn to do that correctly, then they can run while dribbling. If it appears they will always be small in size, then keep working on this with them over and over. Some of the best dribblers and ball handlers ever, took the ball with them everywhere they went and just kept dribbling, and dribbling, and dribbling.

Teaching Techniques

The dribbling skills and drills are numbered so that you can have your assistant coach(s) use them and become more familiar with them for reference purposes. These skill activities will cover the very basic fundaments. We will also try to cover some of the little special techniques that will help them dribble the ball. The plan is stay with small training groups, where you or one of your coaches is teaching one of these techniques or drills. Keep the time period short, maybe 10 to 15 minutes on the group to group (stations) activities. Then blow a whistle and each group moves over to the next group or station.

The size of your groups will depend on how many kids you have in your training session, and how many instructors (coaches) you have. As an example if you have 16 kids on your team, then you could have 4 groups of 4, each learning a different dribbling skill. You will probably need at least 4 assistants or parents helping to pull off this type of training. The bigger your group is though the more problems you will have. Smaller groups mean more touches, and more teaching control on your part. However, some drills may need to be combined for bigger groups in order to teach similar combination player techniques more smoothly and quicker. If you can find them, have an instructor and an assistant at each group or station, then show them exactly what you want them to do. That's the key word *EXACTLY*.

Many coaches don't like to do this, even if they may need to, because of a to many groups, and they may feel they don't have control. However, using parents as assistants and showing them exactly what you want them to do can work. I do this all the time and it works great for me with young kids. Parents are usually just sitting around watching with nothing to do anyway, so why not get them involved and put them to work. You would be surprised at how many parents are willing to help, not a lot of them but quite a few. And that's all you need. The trick is just show them *EXACTLY* what you want them to do

The Basic Dribble Training (No.30)

Object of the activity: Teach all your players how to dribble the basketball.

What you will need: You will need a little room on the court, a basketball, one coach, and some tape to put on the floor, and a whistle.

The Basics Are:

Dribbling is when a player uses one hand to bounce the basketball continuously, without interruption. The dribble ends when this action is interrupted, such as holding the ball when it comes up to the players hand. It ends by grabbing it with both hands, or placing the hand at the side, on the lower half of the ball, or underneath, then rotating the hand before pushing the ball down, and starting to dribble again. In other words if you do not redirect the ball towards the floor after it touches your hand in any way, the dribble has ended. When the dribble has ended, you **can not** hesitate, then start to dribble again. You have to immediately stop, stand in the same place and pass the ball to someone else or shoot.

The correct stance for learning how to dribble is, start by standing in the upright position and stay in one place. Then if you are right handed, your left foot should staggered out in front of your right foot, with both feet parallel to each other *(SEE FIGURE 30)*. Your knees should be bent slightly, and ball in hand. The upper arm is close to the body, and the lower arm is extended out to the ball. Now you are ready to push the ball down to the floor. If you are left handed, everything is just the opposite, with the right foot out in front of the left. All players should know how to dribble. But mostly "Point Guards", and "Shooting Guards", need to work on their basics when they are starting out because they are the players that have to move the ball around.

Working the activity: It might be a good idea to make a 2-1/2 foot square, or a circle the same size, for young kids to start out practicing in. Use tape to make this on the basketball court floor, or use cones to mark the area. Then have your son or daughter stand in this area, and get into the correct stance for right, or left, handed dribbling. Next with ball in hand, have them slowly dribble in place. Make sure they stay inside the area. When they are just starting out, it's ok to have them look at where they are dribbling the ball when they are a beginner. Once they demonstrate they can do this correctly, they can move on to the ball handling moves.

FIGURE 30

Emphasize; using the finger tips only. This will not be easy to do, but they have to learn.
Run this activity: for about 10 minutes making sure each player gets as many touches on the ball as possible. If players are not catching on have an assistant coach pull them aside and show them what they are doing wrong so that the practice does not stop and keeps going.

Either Hand Dribble Training (No.31)
Object of the activity: Teach all your players how to dribble the basketball using either hand.
What you will need: You will need a little room on the court, a basketball, one coach, and a whistle.
The Basics Are: The same as in activity drill 30. **Teach them to dribble with either hand**. If you start teaching them young, they can learn how to do this. When they can dribble with either hand, it makes them twice as hard to guard. If the person guarding a player notices that they only dribble with the one hand, they could over play you towards the side you are dribbling on. Then they could make a steal, or this could force them away from the direction they want to go. Bend the knees, stay low to protect the ball *(SEE FIGURE 31),* and tell them don't look at the ball. All players should be able to dribble with either hand. Even big tall kids can learn how to do this if you start working with them when they are young. But mostly "Point Guards", "Shooting Guards", and "Small Forwards", need to work on this drill.
Working the activity: To start out, have them stand in place and dribble about 10 or 15 times with the strong hand. Then switch and dribble about 10 or 15 times with the weak hand. Then when they get better with either hand, have them dribble out about 20 feet away, switch hands and dribble back to the starting point with the opposite hand. A *TIP* here is, have them dribble with their weakest hand when they are out practicing. This will probably be their left hand if they are right handed, and their right hand if they are left handed. Watch them, and make sure they stay low, and see they don't look at the ball.

FIGURE 31

Emphasize; using the finger tips only. Then how to turn and switch hands.

Run this activity: for about 10 minutes making sure each player gets as many touches on the ball as possible. If players are not catching on have an assistant coach pull them aside and show them what they are doing wrong.

No Look Dribble Training (No.32)

Object of the activity: Teach all your players how to dribble the basketball using either hand and without looking down at the ball.

What you will need: You will need a little room on the court, a basketball, one coach, and a whistle.

The Basics Are; the same as in activity drill 30, except dribbling the basketball without looking at the ball. Teach them, **don't watch the ball as they dribble** *(SEE FIGURE 31)*. When they are first starting out, you will have to really watch them to make sure they don't look. It's learning to feel the ball with their finger tips. I guess you could say, it might be similar to typing, without looking at the keyboard. All players should be able to "no look" dribble. But mostly "Point Guards", and "Shooting Guards", need to work on this drill.

Working the activity: A good way to teach them this lesson is you stand out about 6 or 7 feet in front of them, and hold up anywhere from one to five fingers. And have your hand raised up in the air. Then have them dribble the ball while standing in place. Next as they are dribbling it in front of them, they have to watch you, and see how many fingers you are holding up. To keep telling you how many fingers you are holding up, they have to look up and take their eyes off the ball, in order see your fingers. Then after they have been doing this drill for awhile, have them keep standing still in the same place while continuing to dribble the ball. Then you move around them in a circle, holding up your fingers. They can turn their head to look, but not their feet. Then last of all after they have been doing all of these drills for awhile, have them try to dribble the ball 5 or 6 straight times, and with their eyes closed.

Emphasize; using the finger tips only. Then how to turn and switch hands.

Run this activity: for about 10 minutes making sure each player gets as many touches on the ball as possible. If players are not catching on have an assistant coach pull them aside and show them what they are doing wrong.

Controlled Half Court Dribbling Drill (No.33)

Object of the activity: Teach all your players how to dribble the basketball using either hand over long distances.

What you will need: You will need the full basketball court, two basketballs, two coaches, and two whistles.

The Basics Are; the same as in activity drill 30-32, except dribbling over longer distances All players should be able to dribble and with either hand. But mostly "Point Guards", and "Shooting Guards", need a lot of work on this drill.

Working the activity: Your team is divided into two groups lined up on the base line. The little kids go half court and the bigger kids full court. Have both P1 and P4 first "power" dribble down to the half court line (or full court) and then back going as fast as they can. When they get almost back they pass the ball of to the next player in line who dribbles down and back. When it gets back to P1 and P4 again they "cross over" dribble down and back the next time. Then "stop-N-go", and then "switch hands" the next time. Right handers use their left hand and left handers their right hand. Keep the drill moving so that each player gets to go down and back at least once with each of the 4 types of dribbling.

Emphasize; using the finger tips only. Then how to turn and switch hands.

Run this activity: for about 10 minutes making sure each player gets as many touches on the ball as possible. If players are not catching on have an assistant coach pull them aside and show them what they are doing wrong.

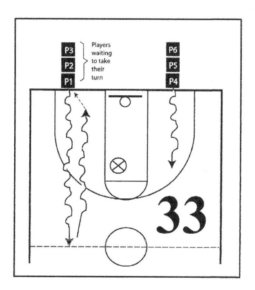

Wave Switch Dribbling Drill (No.34)

Object of the activity: Teach all your players how dribble in traffic as they go around other players or objects.

What you will need: You will need a full court, as many chairs as you can get, two basketballs, two coaches, and two whistles.

The Basics Are: This is a drill to work on all of the different types of dribbles to use in traffic situations.

Working the activity: Your team is divided into two groups lined up on the base line. The little kids go half court and the bigger kids full court. This is just like drill No.33 except the players weave around chairs staggered out in front of them. As they go around each chair to a different side they cross over and switch hands so that the dribble hand is always the hand away from the chair. They dribble down to the half court line for the little kids and full court for the bigger kids. Keep the drill moving so that each player gets to go down and back at least 2 times. You can walk the little kids through it at first then speed it up little by little as they get better. The goal is to get everyone running it fast. Use as many folding chairs as you need. If you can't find chairs use other players or coaches standing still. Or you can just have one line if you are short chairs, players, and coaches.

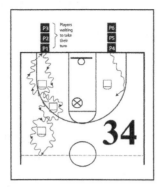

Emphasize; using their fingers, turning, and switching hands.

Run this activity: for about 15 -20 minutes making sure each player gets as many attempts as possible but at least two. If players are not catching on have an assistant coach pull them aside and show them what they are doing wrong so that the practice does not stop and keeps going.

Man to Man Zigzag Dribbling Drill (No.35)

Object of the activity: Teach all your players how to zigzag dribble in traffic as they try to get around other players or.

What you will need: You will need a full court, as many chairs as you can get, two to four basketballs, four coaches, and four whistles.

The Basics Are: This is a drill to work on all of the different types of dribbles that are necessary to use in traffic situations with other players guarding them.

Working the activity: Have your players pair off along the side of the court. On one side is the dribblers (P1,P2) with the ball. Opposite of them are the defenders (P3,P4). There are 3 speeds to this drill. Walking, half speed, and full speed. P1 and P2 zigzag dribble from sideline to sideline. P3 and P4 move right straight at them at the same speed. As they meet P3 and P4 uses a defensive stance and tries to force the P1 and P2 to go around them, shuffling back and forth. They have to stay right with the P1 and P2 as they zig and zag across court. P3 and P4 can't steal the ball and the P1 and P2 can't run into them or blow past them. When they all reach the far side sideline they switch positions. P3 and P4's job is to just keep themselves between P1 or P2 and the sideline behind them. If P1 or P2 beats P3 or P4, then they have to turn around, sprint back and get in front of the them again. This is called a "turn and go". When they get to a full speed run P1 and P2 still have to zig and zag their way across court. Run a walk through first, then a half speed, then a full speed.

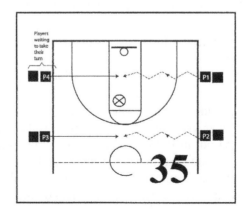

Emphasize; using their fingers, turning, and switching hands.

Run this activity: for about 15 -20 minutes making sure each player gets as many attempts as possible but at least two. If players are not catching on have an assistant coach pull them aside and show them what they are doing wrong so that the practice does not stop and keeps going.

Full Court Throw and Go Dribbling Drill (No.36)

Object of the activity: Teach all your players how to catch a pass and speed dribble (a break away) all the way down to the other end of the court and make a lay up.

What you will need: You will need a full court, two basketballs, two coaches, and one whistle.

The Basics Are: This is a drill to work on catching a long pass, then fast dribbling all the way down to the other end of the court, making a layup, sprinting up court to mid court on the other side, catching another pass, then dribbling in for another lay up.

Working the activity: Have your players line up on one end of the court. The first player P1 sprints towards mid court. P2 throws them a long pass when they get about 1/3 of the way down the court. They catch the pass then speed dribble in for a lay up basket. Next they sprint up to mid court on the other side. P3 gets the rebound and throws them a long pass to mid court. They catch the pass and dribble in to the other basket for a lay up, then go to the end of the line. A new P1 comes up and the drill repeats. Don't forget to rotate P2 and P3 passing players once in a while so that they get to dribble.

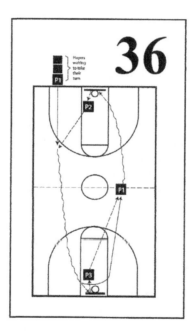

Emphasize; catching the pass and ball control into the basket.

Run this activity: for about 30 minutes making sure each player gets as many attempts as possible but at least two. If players are not catching on have an assistant coach pull them aside and show them what they are doing wrong so that the practice does not stop and keeps going.

10. BALL HANDLING

Note: The ball handling training and drills will be numbered for "EASY " reference.

Ball handling is another very important part of the game of offensive basketball. As a coach or parent you should start teaching them how to handle the ball as soon as they are 5 years old. It is the number one and probably the hardest skill to learn in basketball. One good thing is, it won't cost too much to get them started, just a basketball and a hard surface is needed. It is a coordination skill, and if they keep working at it they can learn how to do it. Probably the first thing to explain to them about ball handling is, maintaining possession of the ball. For dribbling the number one thing to learn is to **use their fingertips for ball control and not the palm of the hand.** The fingertips is where the control comes from. And coaches here is a tip for you, the more they dribble the better they will get, and the better they get the more confidence they will have. Another tip, if you want to see how good they are doing then when you see they have been out practicing, then check their hands. The fingertips should be dirty and the palms clean. They should learn also to **keep the bouncing ball close to them**. If you watch the good dribblers, the ball will be like a Yo-Yo on a string as they move around with it. For the best way to start out practicing dribbling with them is see section 9 on dribbling

There are several moves they can make to keep the ball away from a defender trying to steal it. These are moves like;
- Hesitate or stutter step dribbling,
- Behind the back dribble
- Switch hands crossover dribbling
- Through the legs dribbling
- Spin move dribbling
- Shuffle dribbling
- Stop and go dribbling
- Change of pace dribbling
- Behind the back dribbling and passing

Teaching Techniques
The ball handling skills and drills are numbered so that you can have your assistant coach(s) use them and become more familiar with them for reference purposes. These skill activities will cover the very basic fundaments. We will also try to cover some of the little special techniques that will help them handle the ball. The plan is stay with small training groups, where you or one of your coaches is teaching one of these techniques or drills. Keep the time period short, maybe 10 to 15 minutes on the group to group (stations) activities. Then blow a whistle and each group moves over to the next group or station.

The size of your groups will depend on how many kids you have in your training session, and how many instructors (coaches) you have. As an example if you have 16 kids on your team, then you could have 4 groups of 4, each learning a different ball handling skill. You will probably need at least 4 assistants or parents helping, to pull off this type of training though. The bigger your group is though the more problems you may have. Smaller groups mean more touches, and more teaching control on you or your coaches part. However, some drills may need to be combined for bigger groups in order to teach similar combination player techniques more smoothly and quicker. If you can find them, have an instructor and an assistant at each group or station, then show them exactly what you want them to do. That's the key word *EXACTLY*.

Many coaches don't like to do this, even if they may need to, because of to many groups, and they may feel they don't have control. However, using parents as assistants and showing them exactly what you want them to do can work. I do this all the time and it works great for me with young kids. Parents are usually just sitting around watching with nothing to do anyway, so why not get them involved and put them to work. You would be surprised at how many parents are willing to help, not a lot of them but quite a few. And that's all you need. The trick is just show them *EXACTLY* what you want them to do

Fast High Speed Dribbling Drill (No.37, 38, 39)

Object of the activity: Teach all your players how to high speed dribble to get away from defenders.

What you will need: You will need a full court, two basketballs, two coaches, and one whistle.

The Basics Are: This is a drill for speed dribbling the ball. Generally speaking when dribbling up court: 1) Stay low and protect the ball when you are in traffic (lots of players around you). 2) The knees are bent a little, and the hand has to stay on top of the ball. The forefinger on the dribbling hand should be pointed straight ahead. 3) When an opponent confronts you, stay in position, and keep your body between the opponent and the ball. When dribbling on a fast break from back court, to get the ball up court, the dribble must be a higher up dribble as compared to the low slow speed dribble. Dribbling low, and bent over, will slow down the speed of the dribble. The ball should come up to about waist high on the dribble. Keep the ball out in front and to the side, so you won't accidently kick it *(SEE FIGURE 37)*. They should be able to dribble at this high speed with either hand. This is because you might have to come into the basket from either side. Mostly "Point Guards", "Shooting Guards", and "Small Forwards", need to work on this drill. All players should know how to basically handle the ball, but especially "Point Guards," and "Shooting Guards," have to work on these skills.

Working the activity: To practice this drill, you will need to find a basketball court, or maybe some corner of a large parking lot. Obviously the basketball court would be better, but it is hard to find one these days that is not being used all the time. Take some cones and set them out to mark an area, about the size of a basketball court, which is 50 feet wide by 84 feet long. To practice the high speed down the court dribble, have them dribble all the way up one side of the court with the right hand, then around and down the other side with the left hand *(SEE FIGURE 38)*. First have them dribble slowly, almost walking up and down. Then when they master the technique, have them speed it up little by little. The ball should always be dribbled, on the outside of the court side. This is to keep your body between the opponent and the ball.

To practice just the high speed explosive dribble to the basket, have them go out to the right side of the half court line *(SEE FIGURE 39)*. If you don't have a court, at home you will have to go way out by the sidewalk, and start from there. Or if you don't have a half court line, measure out a distance of about 40 feet from the basket, to start. Then blow the whistle, and have them fire out using a high speed right handed dribble, and go right to the basket for a layup shot. Make sure they really explode out, at high speed, right from the start. Also make sure the dribble is up to waist high, and they are upright with the head up *(SEE FIGURE 37)*, all the way to the basket until they make their jump. Next have them go over to the left side of the half court line, and explode dribble to the basket with the left hand.

FIGURE 37

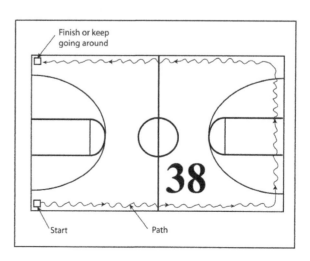

Finish or keep going around

Start

Path

38

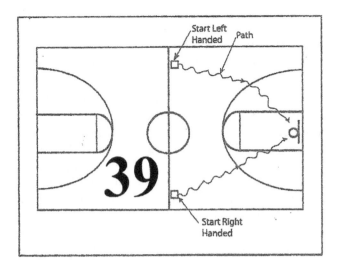

Emphasize; exploding out fast

Run this activity: for about 20 minutes making sure each player gets as many attempts as possible but at least two. If players are not catching on have an assistant coach pull them aside and show them what they are doing wrong so that the practice does not stop and keeps going.

The Hesitate or Stutter Step Dribbling Drill (No.40)

Object of the activity: Teach all your players how to dribble using the hesitate or stutter step technique.

What you will need: You will need some area on the court, a basketball, one coach, a defender, and a whistle.

The Basics Are: In this type of dribble, the dribbler comes at an opponent at a fast dribble. When they get a few yards away from the opponent, they slow down very quickly (the hesitate) and take 3 or 4 short (the stutter) choppy steps *(SEE FIGURE 40-A)*. At this point, don't let the ball come up higher than your hip. The opponent thinks they are going to slow down, so they slow down. The stutter step is actually a faking move. Then all of a sudden, you stay low and fast break explode around them, staying close to them. Then shielding the ball with your body as you go by *(SEE FIGURE 40-B)*. Mostly "Point Guards", and "Shooting Guards", need to work on this drill.

Working the activity: To practice this To practice this drill you, mom or dad, go out to the driveway, or on the court. Then have your players get about 6 or 7 yards away from you. Have them start to dribble very fast right at you. When they start their dribble, you go slowly right towards them, and confront them. What they have to do is, get up to about 8 feet away from you, then slow down quickly. They keep the ball low, no higher than their hip. Next they keep dribbling the ball, but they take 3 or 4 short choppy steps with the feet. This is where the feet speed up, but the dribble speed stays the same. Then all of a sudden, they fast break explode dribble around you. Since they are the one practicing, you have to stand there and let them get by. Observe and make sure they stay low, pivot their body away from you as they go by, and keep their hand on top of the ball. Also make sure they stay very close to you as they go by. Have them come at you first from your right, with a left handed dribble. Try that a few times then have them move over to the other side, and come at you with a right handed dribble. The stutter step is going to be hard for the younger kids to learn. So walk them through it slowly until they catch onto the technique.

A   **FIGURE 40**   B

Emphasize; exploding out fast after stutter stepping.

Run this activity: for about 15 minutes making sure each player gets as many attempts as possible but at least two. If players are not catching on have an assistant coach pull them aside and show them what they are doing wrong so that the practice does not stop and keeps going.

The Behind the Back Dribbling Drill (No.41)

Object of the activity: Teach all your players how to dribble behind their back to get away from a defender.

What you will need: You will need some room on the court, a basketball, one coach, and a whistle.

The Basics Are: This is a drill to work on dribbling behind the back to get away from a defender. They are dribbling along *(SEE FIGURE 41-A)*, then suddenly they push the ball around behind their back, just after it bounces up to their dribble hand *(SEE FIGURE 41-B)*. They execute the rest of this move, by catching it with the other hand as the ball comes around their back to the other side, then bounces up *(SEE FIGURE 41-C)*, so they can keep right on dribbling the ball with the left hand *(SEE FIGURE 41-D)*. This could also be a bounce pass to a teammate nearby. If they are right handed, they push the ball around their waist, to in back of their left hip. If they are left handed, then just the opposite, they push it around with the left hand. Have your players learn to practice this move without looking. Its not easy to do, so it will take a lot of practice. It has to be accomplished mostly by feel, and trial and error attempts. Start when they are young, and keep working with them until they master this technique. Mostly "Point Guards," and "Shooting Guards," need to work on this drill.

Working the activity: To practice this drill, you will need to find a court, or at least a flat driveway to work on. It's probably best to *"walk"* your players through this first, just so they get the feel of what is required. Start by having them go down to one end of the court, or driveway. First have them take the ball with the right hand, then step out with the left foot, and at the same time start to dribble the ball once with the right hand. Next as they start to step out with the right foot, and the ball comes up into the hand, they grasp it with a cupped hand and fingers, from on top of the ball. Then they roll push it behind your back. As it comes around, they push it downward at an angle, and let it drop to the floor just outside of their left thigh. Some coaches like to call this a "slap your left butt cheek" action. Then as the ball is about to hit the floor, they start to step forward with their left foot. And then when the ball bounces up, they catch it with the left hand and dribble it down once. Next when it comes back up, they roll it back around their back with the left hand, just like with the right hand. The object is to move slowly straight down the court, switching hands as they go behind your back. What they want to eventually do in this drill is, get a fluid motion going. One dribble on the right, then behind their back, one dribble on the left, then behind their back. They should be doing this as they walk forward, all the way down the court. When they have mastered this technique, you can have them speed up the drill, little by little. It will take many hours, and lots of patience on your part to teach them to perform this move smoothly. It's one of the hardest moves to learn, in basketball. And some kids may never learn how to do it until they get older. If they get real frustrated, just quit working on this drill and come back to it later. Even if they can't learn this move, they can still be a good "Point Guard," or a "Shooting Guard."

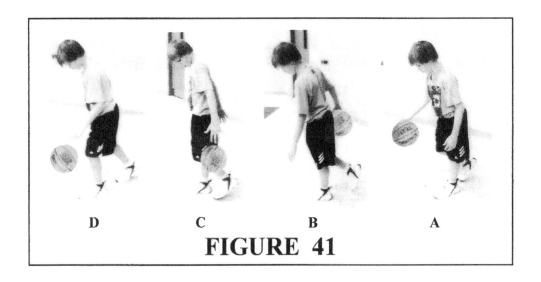

FIGURE 41

Emphasize; coordinating the dribble and the switching hands part of the move.

Run this activity: for about 15 minutes making sure each player gets as many attempts as possible but at least two. If players are not catching on have an assistant coach pull them aside and show them what they are doing wrong so that the practice does not stop and keeps going.

The Switch Hands Crossover Dribbling Drill (No.42)

Object of the activity: Teach all your players how to make the switch hands crossover dribble to get away from a defender.

What you will need: You will need some room on the court, a basketball, one coach, and a whistle.

The Basics Are: The ball is dribbled down court, switching it from one side to the other, and then from one hand to the other. When they have mastered this technique, it can be done at moderate to high speed. Changing pace while executing this dribbling move, will confuse and fool the opponent also. When dribbled, the ball needs to be pushed down keeping it close to the body, and always toward the back foot side. And as you push the ball across, keep it no higher than the top of the knee. Another part of this technique is, changing direction along with the crossover. This move is used to get around an opponent, from back court to the middle of the court. Mostly "Point Guards," "Shooting Guards," and "Small Forwards," need to work on this drill.

Working the activity: To practice this drill, you will need to find a court, or at least a flat driveway to work on. It's probably best to *"walk"* your players through this first, just so they get the feel of what is required. Start by having them go down to one end of the court, or driveway. First have them take the ball with the right hand, then step out with the right foot *(SEE FIGURE 42-A)*. And next, at the same time, dribble push the ball in one dribble, across the front of their body *(SEE FIGURE 42-B)*, so it comes up to their left hand. Their left foot should hit the floor as they step out with the ball, just as the ball has come up to their left hand *(SEE FIGURE 42-C)*.

Next repeat the move, from your left hand bouncing it across to your right hand. Then keep repeating the move, back and forth as you walk down the court. With the young kids, they can look down at the ball until they master the technique. Eventually though they need to speed up the drill, all the way down the court, little by little as they get better at performing the move. And they should also work towards _not_ looking at the ball while making this move. The key is perfecting the footwork, timing, and speed of the move.

C   B   A

FIGURE 42

Emphasize; coordinating the bounce with the hand switching.

Run this activity: for about 15 minutes making sure each player gets as many attempts as possible but at least two. If players are not catching on have an assistant coach pull them aside and show them what they are doing wrong so that the practice does not stop and keeps going.

Through the Legs Dribbling Drill (No.43)

Object of the activity: Teach all your players how to make the through the legs dribble to get away from a defender.

What you will need: You will need some room on the court, a basketball, one coach, and a whistle.

The Basics Are: The through the legs dribble is really a variation of the crossover dribble. The ball is pushed between the legs, instead of in front of the body. When it comes out the other side, you start to dribble with the other hand, then go in the opposite direction. You need to bend down and stay low, just before you push the ball between your legs. A little head fake, off to the side "opposite" of where you really want to go, will help the move be even more successful. In a way though this move may be a better choice than the crossover dribble move because even if the opponent is close to you, it's harder for them to reach the ball when it goes between the legs. And it's a good change of pace move, in the front court, to get you into the lane for a shot. Mostly "Point Guards," and "Shooting Guards," need to work on this drill.

Working the activity: To practice this drill, you will need to find a court, or at least a flat driveway to work on. It's probably best to *"walk"* your players through this first, just so they get the feel of what is required. You can have them speed things up, little by little as the get better, and more comfortable with the technique. There are several ways to make this move. Have them try out both ways, then start out using the one that is easiest for them to execute. The first is, start by having them go down to one end of the court, or driveway. Have them take the ball with the right hand, then as they start to dribble, step out with their left foot at about a 45 degree angle towards their left *SEE FIGURE 43-A)*. Stay low with the knees bent a little. Next just as their left foot is about to hit the floor, they bounce push the ball under and through the left leg *(SEE FIGURE 43-B)*. While they are doing this, place their left hand behind them, with the palm facing their back. This is so they are ready to catch the ball as it comes through. Then just as they are catching the ball, with their left hand, step forward and to the right, at a 45 degree angle with their right foot. This is to make room, for a smooth transition of the ball under their legs. Then they bring the ball around their left foot, and start to dribble off to their left *(SEE FIGURE 43-C)*. This move will be a little unnatural for them when they start, but keep working at it until they get used to it. This is the better of the two moves if you want to change the direction they are going in. Next they dribble the ball several times as they are dribbling and walking, then reverse the process and bounce push the ball back under their legs to the right hand. Have them keep doing this back and forth all the way down the court. Two or three dribbles, then change hands.

The second is, start by having them go down to one end of the court, or driveway. Have them take the ball with the right hand, then as they start to dribble, take a big step straight ahead with their left foot *(SEE FIGURE 43-A)*. At the same time bend the right leg down at the knee. Next bounce push the ball under and through the left leg *(SEE FIGURE 43-B)*. At the same time place the left hand, with the palm down, next to their left thigh. This is to catch the ball with the left hand as it comes up. Then as they step straight ahead with the right foot, they bring the ball around their left foot, and start to dribble off straight ahead. Except now the ball is on their left side away from the opponent *(SEE FIGURE 43-C)*. This is the best move if they want to keep going basically straight ahead, and keep the ball away from their opponent who is on their right side. Next they dribble the ball several times as they are dribbling and walking, then reverse the process, and bounce push the ball back under their legs to their right hand. They keep doing this, back and forth, all the way down the court. Two or three dribbles, then change hands.

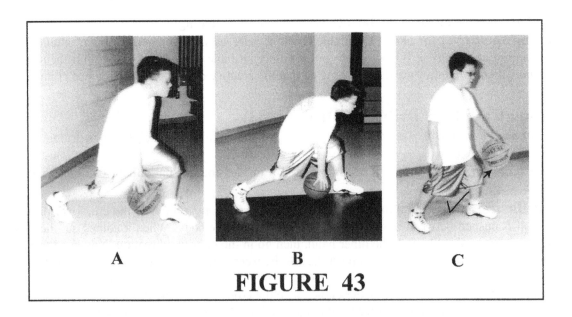

A   B   C

FIGURE 43

Emphasize; coordinating the bounce with the hand switching between the legs.
Run this activity: for about 15 minutes making sure each player gets as many attempts as possible but at least two. If players are not catching on have an assistant coach pull them aside and show them what they are doing wrong so that the practice does not stop and keeps going.

The Spin Move Dribbling Drill (No.44)

Object of the activity: Teach all your players how to make the spin move dribble to get away from defenders.

What you will need: You will need a full court, a basketball, one coach, and one whistle.

The Basics Are: The spin move dribble is a spin around, change direction move. While you are dribbling straight ahead, you spin around in a reverse pivot. Then change to the opposite hand as you go around, and then go off in another direction. The ball should be kept close to the body, and swing the head around fast. Mostly "Point Guards," "Shooting Guards," and "Small Forwards," need to work on this drill.

Working the activity: To practice this drill, you will need to find a court, or at least a flat driveway to work on. It's probably best to *"walk"* your players through this first, just so they get the feel of what is required. You can have them speed things up little by little as the get better, and more comfortable with the technique.

Start by having them go down to one end of the court, or driveway. Have them take the ball with the right hand, then as they start to dribble slowly towards you, they take one jab step right at you with the left foot as they get about 6 feet away *(SEE FIGURE 44-A)*. Next they have to stop very quickly, reverse pivot spin around to their right. The spin around should go about 3/4 of the way around. As they spin, they keep the ball close to the body *(SEE FIGURE 44-B)*. And the head spin around should be done very quickly, almost a snapping motion. When they start the spin around, they push the ball down, then they spin and catch it with the left hand *(SEE FIGURE 44-B)* as it comes up fom the dribble. Then they continue the spin while dribbling off to the left at a slight angle with the left hand *(SEE FIGURE 44-C)*. Next dribble the ball several times in the left hand as you are dribbling and walking down the court, then reverse the process, jab step with the right foot, spin around to your left, and change the dribble to the right hand. Keep doing this, back and forth, all the way down the court. Two or three dribbles, spin, then change hands. To make this work the spin has to executed very fast.

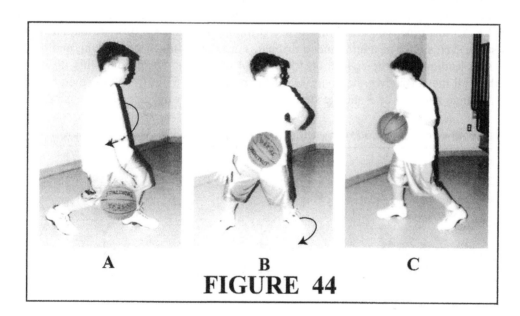

A   **B**   **C**

FIGURE 44

Emphasize; the fast head spin and foot pivot.

Run this activity: for about 15 minutes making sure each player gets as many attempts as possible but at least two. If players are not catching on have an assistant coach pull them aside and show them what they are doing wrong so that the practice does not stop and keeps going.

The Shuffle Dribbling Drill (No.45)

Object of the activity: Teach all your players how to make the shuffle dribble to get away from defenders.

What you will need: You will need some room on the court, a basketball, one coach, and one whistle.

The Basics Are: The shuffle dribble is sort of a straight ahead, sliding, advancing, shuffle move, first with one foot then the other while dribbling the ball. You remember the phrase "Inching ahead cautiously". Well that is kind of like what this is, except you are going a little farther than inching. This would be a move you might use in the front court, to kind of slowly move toward the basket when the opponent is fronting you, but backed off a little bit. Mostly "Point Guards," "Shooting Guards," and "Small Forwards," need to work on this drill.

Working the activity: To practice this drill, you will need to find a court, or at least a flat driveway to work on. It's probably best to *"walk"* your players through this first, just so they get the feel of what is required. You can have them speed things up, little by little as the get better, and feel more comfortable with the technique. Start by having them go down to one end of the court, or driveway. Have them stand straight up, with feet apart about shoulder width. Your left foot and your head should be pointing straight ahead. Then rotate your body to the right until your left shoulder is pointing straight ahead also. Turn the right foot 90 degrees, so it is pointing to the right. Next bend at the knees to about a 45 degree angle to the floor, and widen your stance out about another 6 inches. Then move the left arm straight out from your body at about a 45 degree angle, then bend the forearm so it is at a right angle from the upper arm. They take the ball in their right hand. At this point, they are ready to start shuffle dribbling down the court *(SEE FIGURE 45-A)*. Make sure their knees are bent, and they dribble no higher than the knees. The point they bounce the ball on the dribble, should be halfway between the front foot and the back foot. One more thing, the forefinger on the dribble hand should be pointed in the direction you are shuffling. Start to dribble with the right hand, and at the same time slide step out with your left foot *(SEE FIGURE 45-B)*. The second the left foot stops, slide step straight ahead with the turned right foot, bringing it up close to the left foot while still pointing it to the right *(SEE FIGURE 45-C)*. All this time, you are bent low and dribbling the ball. Do this straight ahead for about 4 or 5 steps, then switch to a left handed dribble. Turn the shoulder to the right, and do the same shuffle step leading with the right foot, for about 4 or 5 steps. Keep doing this, from one side to the other, all the way down the court. Have them take 4 or 5 shuffle steps, then turn the opposite way, change hands, 4 or 5 shuffle steps, turn the opposite wayagain, change hands, and so on.

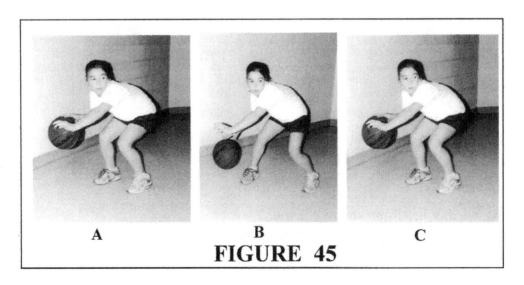

A   B   C

FIGURE 45

Emphasize; the short shuffle steps while protecting the ball.

Run this activity: for about 15 minutes making sure each player gets as many attempts as possible but at least two. If players are not catching on have an assistant coach pull them aside and show them what they are doing wrong so that the practice does not stop and keeps going.

The Change of Pace Dribbling Drill (No.46)

Object of the activity: Teach all your players how to make the change of pace dribble to get away from defenders.

What you will need: You will need some room on the court, a basketball, one coach, and one whistle.

The Basics Are: The change of pace dribble is a variation of the "stop and go" dribble. If you dribble at a constant speed, it is easier for the opponent to guard you. All they have to do is match your speed, and they stay right with you. So what you do is vary the rate of speed of the dribble. When they match your speed, you slow down quickly when they slow down you speed up quickly. I have heard some people call this the "Yo-Yo effect". Mostly "Point Guards," "Shooting Guards," and "Small Forwards," need to work on this drill.

Working the activity: To practice this drill, you will need to find a court, or at least a large flat driveway, or even a parking lot, to practice on. It's probably best to *"walk"* your players through this first, just so they get the feel of what is required. You can have them speed things up, little by little as the get better, and feel more comfortable with the technique. We will use the basketball court as our guide. However if you don't have a court to use, then mark off equivalent distances with cones. Start by having them go down to one end of the court on the base line, or end of the driveway, or a marked off place with cones on the parking lot. Have them start with a fast high speed "right" handed dribble, going down court *(SEE FIGURE 46-A)*. Then you or a coach get right next to them, but not too close, and try to match the speed at which they are moving. What you want to have them do is, all of a sudden after dribbling about 5 yards down court, have them slow down very quickly, but don't come to a stop *(SEE FIGURE 46-B)*. You slow down with them. What they have to do is watch you, and when they see you slow down, they speed up *(SEE FIGURE 46-C)*. Then you speed up, and try to stay next to them. Again they have to watch you, out of the corner of their eyes. When they see that you are really coming hard to catch them, they slow down and let you catch them, then when you slow down again, they speed up again. This goes on all the way down to the other base line. The object is to keep you from staying right along side of them where you could reach in and knock the ball away from them. Now, both of you stop at the base line, turn around, and have them go down the court doing the same thing the other way, except dribbling this time with their "left" hand. The tip here is, keep doing this over and over again. In other words, practice, practice, practice.

C   B   A

FIGURE 46

Emphasize; using the defender to judge their stop and go.

Run this activity: for about 15 minutes making sure each player gets as many attempts as possible but at least two. If players are not catching on have an assistant coach pull them aside and show them what they are doing wrong so that the practice does not stop and keeps going.

11. OFFENSIVE PLAYS

Note: All offensive plays will be numbered for "EASY " reference. See page 8 legend for player numbering explanation shown on all diagrams..

Simple Basic Offensive Plays

The Give and Go Play *(No.1)*

Object of the play: Teach your players how to use the "Stop and Go" play to go to the basket and score.

What you will need: You will need nearly the full court, a basketball, 5 offensive players, 5 defenders, two coaches, and one whistle.

How the play works: Get all your players, except No.5, quickly up court. Try to get the opposition to think you are moving towards the left corner. Have your No.4 player get the oppositions No. 4 player to follow them to the right corner of the court by waving their arm for a pass. When that starts to happen, have your No.1 player pass the ball to your No.5 player at the top of the key (the Give), who then fakes turning to their right, then turns back to their left and passes back to No. 1 breaking up court past them as they go by. No.1 then goes directly to the basket for a lay-up (the Go). You can also flip flop, or go to the opposite side, with this same play.

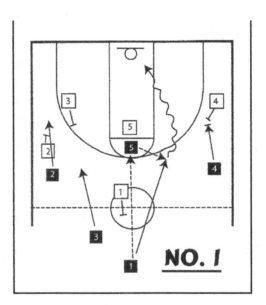

Working the Practice: Put all 10 players in position and run the play with No.1 bringing up the ball. Just for practice have the defender covering No.4 pretend to chase them into the corner. When No.5 gets the ball they make a quick fake pass to No.4 in the corner. With the young kids you may need to walk through this several time to make sure everyone knows their part.

Emphasize; the fake to No.4 to get the defender thinking they will get the pass which leaves the lane open for No.1 on the "GO."

Run this Play: for about 20 minutes. Getting as many run thru's as possible. If some players are not catching on to their part in the play, substitute and have an assistant coach pull them aside and show them what they are doing wrong so that the practice does not stop and keeps going.

The Pick and Roll Play *(No.2)*

Object of the play: Teach your players how to use the "Pick and Roll" play to go to the basket and score.

What you will need: You will need at least half the court, a basketball, 5 offensive players, 5 defenders, two coaches, and one whistle.

How the play works: Your player No.1 gets the ball to the left of the lane, then starts to dribble toward the top of the key. At that same time your player No.5 moves over to screen out the oppositions player No.1 (the PICK). Then player No. 1 can do several things. If they are clear to go around the screen, and past the oppositions player No.5, then they dribble to the basket for a lay-up. If the oppositions No.5 comes over to seal them off from the basket, then your player No.5 rolls and breaks to the basket (the ROLL). Your No.1 bounce passes them the ball for a lay up. If both the oppositions players No.1 and 5 go to seal off No.1, they still pass to No. 5 for a lay-up.

Working the Practice: Put all 10 players in position and run the play with No.1 getting the ball out by the left 3-point circle. Just for practice have the defenders No. 5 and No.3 Not chase or cover No.5 so that they get practice on the roll. With the young kids you may need to walk through this several time to make sure everyone knows their part. Practice this play to the left and then to the right side.

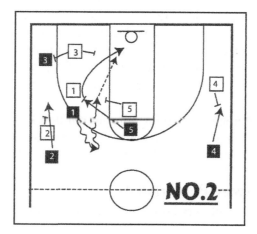

Emphasize; the No.1 player really faking a dribble to the basket in order to get the No.5 defender to come over to cover them. This allows No.5 to get clear on their roll to the basket. This is a very good play, even the Pro's use it a lot.

Run this Play: for about 20 minutes. Getting as many run thru's as possible. If some players are not catching on to their part in the play, substitute and have an assistant coach pull them aside and show them what they are doing wrong so that the practice does not stop and keeps going.

The Back Door Play *(No.3)*

Object of the play: Teach your players how to use the "Back Door" play to go to the basket and score.

What you will need: You will need at least half the court, a basketball, 5 offensive players, 5 defenders, two coaches, and one whistle.

How the play works: your team is bigger, but slow, this could work for you against an aggressive team that overplays the passing lanes. This play is designed to go to your player No.3 around the "back door" as they call it. First your No. 1 player dribbles up into the front court to the top of the 3 point arc. Player No.3 steps to the right side, behind the opposing player No.3. Then your No.1 fakes a pass to your No.3 player. If the opposing No.3 player steps in front to block the pass, your No.3 player then turns and goes to the basket for the back door pass and lay up. This works best when your No.3 player gets behind the opposing No.3 player.

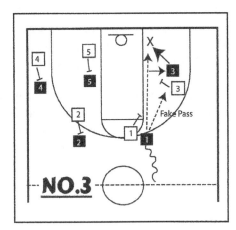

Working the Practice: Put all 10 players in position and run the play with No.1 getting the ball out to the right near the center circle. Then dribbling it in near the top of the key and on the right side of the 3-point circle. Just for practice have the defenders No. 5 and No.3 Not chase or cover No.3 so that they get practice on breaking around to the back door for a jump shot. With the young kids you may need to walk through this several time to make sure everyone knows their part. Practice this play to the right and to the left side, by flip flopping the players positions.

Emphasize; the No.1 player really making a good fake pass over to No.3 out to the right near the 3-point circle.

Run this Play: for about 20 minutes. Getting as many run thru's as possible. If some players are not catching on to their part in the play, substitute and have an assistant coach pull them aside and show them what they are doing wrong so that the practice does not stop and keeps going.

The Pass and Screen Away Play *(No.4)*

Object of the play: Teach your players how to use the "Pass and Screen Away" play to go to the basket and score.

What you will need: You will need at least half the court, a basketball, 5 offensive players, 5 defenders, two coaches, and one whistle.

How the play works: In this play your No.1 player brings the ball up to the top of the key. They then pass the ball to your No.3 player. At the same time your No.4 player moves in a zigzag towards the top of the key, right at your No.1. They pass each other, and as the oppositions No.4 tries to follow your No.4 player, your No.1 player blocks out and screens them. This should free up your No.4 player to get a pass back from No.3 as they break towards the basket for a lay up. Then your No.3 screens out the No.3 defender, hopefully leaving the lane free. This will only work if you can get the opposing team to overload the left side of the court, freeing up the lane for a lay up.

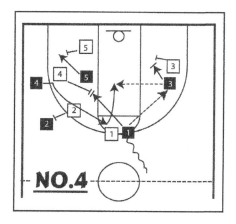

Working the Practice: Put all 10 players in position and run the play with No.1 bringing the ball in from out to the right near the center circle. Then dribbling it in near the top of the key and on the right side of the 3-point circle. Just for practice have the defenders No. 5 and No.4 Not chase or cover No.4 so that they get practice on coming in, and breaking around the screen to the basket for either a lay up or baby jumper. Also practice this play from the left side and screening around to the left side, by flip flopping the players positions.

Emphasize; the No.1 player really making a good screen on No. 4 defender chasing your No.4 coming around on the screen.

Run this Play: for about 20 minutes. Getting as many run thru's as possible. If some players are not catching on to their part in the play, substitute and have an assistant coach pull them aside and show them what they are doing wrong so that the practice does not stop and keeps going.

Zone Offensive Plays

The 1-3-1 Zone Cutter Play *(No.5)*

Object of the play: Teach your players how to use the "1-3-1 Zone Cutter" play to go to the basket and score.

What you will need: You will need at least half the court, a basketball, 5 offensive players, 5 defenders, two coaches, and one whistle.

How the play works: This is a basic play against a 2-3 Zone Defense. Your No.1 player brings the ball up into the front court, to the top of the key. Then they turn and pass to your No.3 player. Your No.3 player then becomes the play maker. They have several options, they can look for your No.5 player as a cutter, either way, on the base line and pass to them, or they can pass to your No.4 breaking into a clear space on the perimeter. This is an overload to the left side play. You can also flip flop it, and overload to the right.

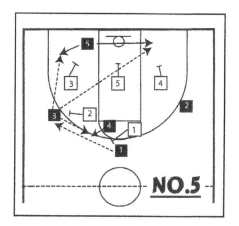

Working the Practice: Put all 10 players in position and run the play with No.1 starting with the ball behind the top of the key. They pass the ball to your No.3 on the left side 3-point circle. Your No.3 then has some options. They can pass to your No.5 out on the flat, or the can pass to No.5 breaking to the other side of the basket. Or they can pass to your No.4 breaking out to the left 3-point circle. The best play is to get the ball to your No.5 breaking to the other weak side of the basket which should open them up to score.

Emphasize; the No.3 player really making a good fake then a pass to your No.5 breaking to the other side of the basket. It's a timing play to get it to work.

Run this Play: for about 20 minutes. Getting as many run thru's as possible. If some players are not catching on to their part in the play, substitute and have an assistant coach pull them aside and show them what they are doing wrong so that the practice does not stop and keeps going.

The 1-3-1 Zone Turn or Fill Play *(No.6)*

Object of the play: Teach your players how to use the "1-3-1 Zone Turn and Fill" play to go to the basket and score.

What you will need: You will need at least half the court, a basketball, 5 offensive players, 5 defenders, two coaches, and one whistle.

How the play works: This is another basic play against a 2-3 Zone Defense. This play probably works best when you have a fairly big center who is a good shooter. Your No.1 player brings the ball up towards the front court. Then they pass the ball to your No.5 center on the hi post. Your No.5 center immediately pivots all the way around and faces the basket. If they have space in front of them, they dribble a few steps then take a jump shot at the basket. If your opponents No.5 player starts to come in and collapse on them , they pass to your No. 4 player, who has filled into the lane behind their No.5 under the basket.

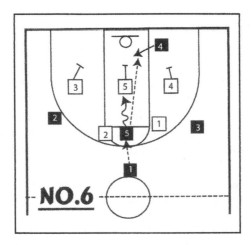

NO.6

Working the Practice: Put all 10 players in position and run the play with No.1, starting with the ball at the edge of the center circle. They pass the ball to your No.5 player at the top of the key. The best play is to get the ball to your No.4 breaking in under the basket for an easy shot.

Emphasize; the No.5 player really making a good decision as to shoot or pass.

Run this Play: for about 20 minutes. Getting as many run thru's as possible. If some players are not catching on to their part in the play, substitute and have an assistant coach pull them aside and show them what they are doing wrong so that the practice does not stop and keeps going.

The 1-3-1 Zone Wings Free Play *(No.7)*

Object of the play: Teach your players how to use the "1-3-1 Zone Wings Free" play to go to the basket and score.

What you will need: You will need at least half the court, a basketball, 5 offensive players, 5 defenders, two coaches, and one whistle.

How the play works: Here is still another play against a 2-3 Zone Defense. This play works by putting your No.5 center at the hi post. Your No.1 player brings the ball up towards the front court. Then they fake a pass to your No.5 center, which usually causes the defense to collapse on your center. After that your center moves to their left. The zone players should rotate around to the right side to follow your center. Your No.1 player then looks to see if your No. 3 player is clear. That look should rotate the zone even more to the right side. Then your No.1 turns and passes to your No. 2 player, who should be open to go to the basket.

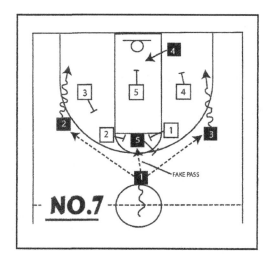

Working the players in position No.1, starting with the ***Practice:*** Put all 10 and run the play with the ball at the edge of the center circle. They fake pass the ball to your No.5 player at the top of the key. The best play may be to get the ball to your No.2 dribbling in under the basket for an easy shot.

Emphasize; the No.1 player really making a good decision as to who pass to.

Run this Play: for about 20 minutes. Getting as many run thru's as possible. If some players are not catching on to their part in the play, substitute and have an assistant coach pull them aside and show them what they are doing wrong so that the practice does not stop and keeps going.

The 1-2-2 Zone Across Court Play *(No.8)*

Object of the play: Teach your players how to use the "1-2-2 Zone Across Court" play to go to the basket and score.

What you will need: You will need at least half the court, a basketball, 5 offensive players, 5 defenders, two coaches, and one whistle.

How the play works: This play can easily shift from a 1-3-1 offense to this 1-2-2 offense. In this case we are showing it against a 2-3 Zone Defense, which is popular for many youth teams to use. Your No.1 player brings the ball up into the front court. Then your No.1 player passes the ball to your No.2 player out on the left wing. This should cause the zone to rotate over to the left side a little. Next your No.2 player passes the ball right back to your No.1 player. Your No.1 player then passes the ball to your No.3 player on the right wing. The opponents zone players then think you are trying to trick them, and they will probably rotate back to the right side. As soon as your No.3 player can see that is happening, they make a long over the top pass back to your No.2 player that has slipped in behind the zone. They take it to the basket or make a short jump shot. Your No.5 moves in and screens out their No.5 or No.3 player, whichever is closest to the basket.

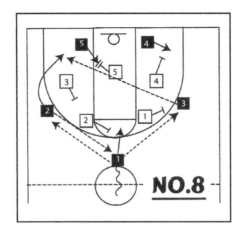

Working the Practice: Put all 10 players in position and run the play, with No.1 starting with the ball at the edge of the center circle. They pass the ball to your No.2 or No.3 players out on the wings. If they pass to your No.3 then No.2 breaks around the left side towards the basket and gets a long pass from No.3. Your No.5 moves up and screens out No.5 defender, and No.2 takes the shot. If they pass the ball to your No.2 then they pass the ball back to No.1 who passes to No.3. Then No.2 breaks towards the basket and your No.5 screens and No. 2 takes the shot.

Emphasize; the No.1 player really making a good decision as to who to pass to, and No.5 making a good screen to clear the shot for No.2.

Run this Play: for about 20 minutes. Getting as many run thru's as possible. If some players are not catching on to their part in the play, substitute and have an assistant coach pull them aside and show them what they are doing wrong so that the practice does not stop and keeps going.

Motion Offensive Plays

Note: These will be easier for your older players. Most 6, 7, and 8 year olds will have a hard time learning and remembering all this motion.

The Arrow Play *(No.12 Thru 15)*

Object of the play: Teach your players how to use the "Arrow" play to create a lot of motion to confuse the defenders. There are four separate motions to this play then they go to the basket.

What you will need: You will need half the court, a basketball, 5 offensive players, 5 defenders, two coaches, and one whistle.

How the first motion (No.12) works: Your No.1 brings the ball up into the front court. Your player No.2 moves up towards the ball. Your No.4 player breaks from the hi-post across the lane down to the left side of the key. Your No.3 turns toward the lane and screens their No.1 until your No. 4 player starts to get through the lane. Then they move quickly to the hi-post, on the right.

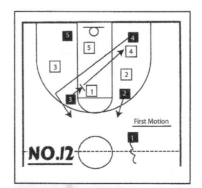

50

How the second motion (No.13) works: Your No.1 passes the ball to your No.4, then breaks up the lane towards the basket. If it's open your No.1 and No.4 work a "give and Go". Then your No.1 dribbles up the lane toward the basket, turns to the right and passes the ball to your No.3. Next No. 1 screens for No.3, who breaks for the basket and makes a lay up or a short jump shot. Your No.5 moves out to the edge of the 3 point circle, pulling their No.3 player with them.

How the third motion (No.14) works: If your No.4 can't work the "give and go" with No.1, they can pass to your No.5, who has moved back over to the edge of the lane. Or if it's open they can follow your No.1 up the lane, and right to the basket. The desired option is to pass to your No.5 player, who is in a better position to go to the basket for a lay up or a jump shot. Your No.1 must get out of the lane before too much time in the lane is called, then quickly move back across the lane to screen out their No. 5 player. If your No. 4 dribbles up the middle, your No.2 has to screen out their No. 2.

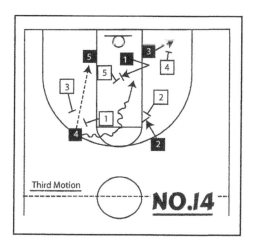

How the fourth motion (No.15) works: If your No.5 can not get open for a shot, they hold the ball. In the mean time, your No.3 has cut back across the lane and curled to the other side, way out on the edge of the 3 point arc as a safety valve. If your No.4 did not dribble up the middle, they fake a cut toward the middle of the lane, and then move back out to the point on the 3 point arc. At this point, your No.5 has to take a shot or pass out to your No.3 or No.4 players. When your No.1 and No.2 players see your No.5 is jammed up and stalling, they pick for each other with No.1 moving down to the free throw line, and No.2 executing a "back door" moving to the lo post. No.2 should be open for a jump shot or a lay up, if so your No.5 passes them the ball. At this point if none of this works, your No.5 passes back out to your No.1 at the free throw line, to reload.

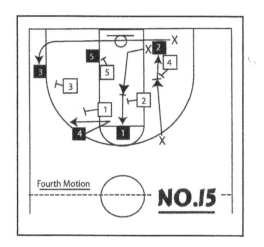

Working the Practice: Put all 10 players in position and run each motion play as shown on the diagram. Make sure to tell the defensive players to act out what they are supposed to do in their positions even though they know the play. The practice is for the offensive players so they must be partially clear to practice the play.

Emphasize; the players needing to make a fake, where necessary, carry it out and make it look good.

Run this Play: for about 30 minutes. Getting as many run thru's as possible. If some players are not catching on to their part in the play, substitute, and have an assistant coach pull them aside and show them what they are doing wrong so that the practice does not stop and keeps going.

Transition Offensive Plays

Note: Your transition offense can be "fast break", or a "walk it up the floor" transition. The fast break can produce easy scores. Moving it up the floor quickly puts a lot of pressure on the defense. To run it you need a fast energetic team. The up tempo game should favor the team that is well conditioned. A team that is maybe bigger and heavier, and not well conditioned, will "run out of gas" so to speak by the third or fourth period. If you have a lot of good fast bench players on your team, it is in your advantage to use the up tempo game. Also getting the ball up the floor quickly before the defense can get set, works good against Zone Defenses. If your team is bigger and slower, then it's in your advantage to walk or bring the ball up court more slowly and methodically. There are *PRIMARY* and *SECONDARY* transition plays

On transitions, have your post players get up the floor quickly when possible, with a guard that is a good ball handler bringing it up the court in back. This leaves room for the guards to maneuver, or maybe throw a long pass if the post player beats the defense up court.

The Primary Fast Break Transition Plays *(No.23 to 27)*

Object of the play: Teach your players how to make a primary fast break on the "transition." There are five separate parts to this to this play including the lanes diagram.

What you will need: You will need the full court, a basketball, 5 offensive players, 2 defenders, two coaches, and one whistle.

How the different lanes (No.23) work:
One of the best ways to run the fast break is, teach your players that there are 3 lanes to come up the court in. One lane is up the middle, and the other two are along the sidelines. The idea is to fill all 3 lanes, not just one or two, as you come up the floor. And as they come up the floor, there is a "trailer" (No.4) and a "prevent" player (No.5). Actually it doesn't matter which 3 players is in which lane up front, just as long as they spread out and fill all 3 lanes as quickly as they can, then GO fast. Usually the "trailer", and the "prevent" player, is designated so they know their role. When it's an outlet play, most coaches say have the outlet pass go to the point guard (No.1). When the outlet pass is after a score, make sure your No.1 is in the middle area of the court to take the pass. When the outlet pass is from a sideline, make sure your No.1 goes to that sideline quickly to take the pass. After your No.1 has received the pass, they dribble and move quickly to the center lane, then come up the court. And if the fast break does not develop, they slow down and bring the ball up slowly to avoid a turnover.

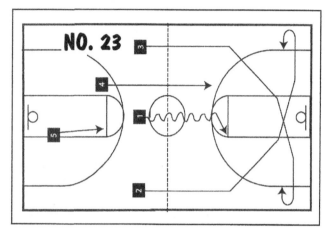

On defensive rebounds, the general rule is the player that gets the rebound is the last player to come up the court. First thing they do is, get the ball to your No.1 in the middle of the court. This is the fastest, easiest, and safest way to get the fast break going. Your No.1 should dribble all the way up to the top of the key before making a pass if possible. The 2 outside lane players cut across the court at 45 degrees (criss cross), and look for a pass from your No.1. If your No.1 stops and makes a jump shot from around the free throw line, the 2 wing players should crash the board for a rebound. The "prevent" player comes up the court slowly, their job is make sure no opponent player gets behind them. That way if an opponent intercepts or steals the ball, they don't have a clear path to the basket.

The 2 on 1 Fast Break First Option No.24
This is when your No.1 finds a "2 on 1" fast break situation, they should take the ball directly to the basket, or get fouled. They should try to attack the basket at an angle, from along the lane line. Their No.2 team mate should take a position on the opposite side, at the lo-post, and watch for a pass or the rebound.

First Option NO.24

The 2 on 1 Fast Break Second Option No.25

This is when your No.1 can see that the defender has come up and is blocking their path to the basket and ready to take a "charging" foul, they pull up and pass to the team mate (No.2), who takes it quickly to the basket for a lay up.

The 3 on 2 Fast Break First Option No.26

This is see where the defenders are set up as you approach the top of the key. As you are coming down the middle of the court, usually one defender will try to stop you at the free throw line. And the second defender will probably be positioned down low right under the basket. If that is the case, your No.1 should not penetrate beyond the free throw line. They stop there and look for either your No.2 or No.3 players driving to the basket. They pass to whichever player is most open. That player tries to dribbles to the basket for a lay up. At this point it is a 2 on 1 situation with the opponents No.3 player. If their No.3 player moves to block your No. 2 player, they pass over to your No.3 player for the lay up.

The 3 on 2 Fast Break Second Option No.27

This is if your No.2 player starts to dribble to the basket, and is blocked by their No.3 who has moved over, they either pass to your No.3 on the other side of the lane or back to your No. 1. If they pass off to your No.1, then No.1 immediately breaks toward the basket for a lay up. If the opponents No.1 moves to a position to block your No.1, they can pass to your No.3 for the lay up.

Working the Practice: Put all 10 players in position and run each primary fast break play as shown on the diagram. Make sure to tell the defensive players to act out what they are supposed to do in their positions even though they know the play. The practice is for the offensive players so they must be at least partially clear to easily practice the play.

Emphasize; the players needing to make a fake, where necessary, carry it out and make it look good.

Run this Play: for about 30 minutes, then come back to it again another day. Getting as many run thru's as possible. If some players are not catching on to their part in the play, substitute, and have an assistant coach pull them aside and show them what they are doing wrong so that the practice does not stop and keeps going.

The Secondary Fast Break Transition Play *(No.28 to 35)*

Note: When a primary fast break is not an option, then run a "secondary fast break". When you have a secondary fast break play, it helps a lot in getting quick baskets in transition.

Motion Secondary Break

This is a little different type of fast break to use when your players get into the front court. Even if the defense gets back quickly, this gives you some good scoring chances.

Object of the play: Teach your players how to make a secondary fast break on the "transition." There are eight separate parts to this to this play.

What you will need: You will need the full court, a basketball, 5 offensive players, a couple of defenders if you need them, two coaches, and one whistle.

How the positioning works:

Motion No.1 First Option No.28

The inbounds pass should go quickly to your No.1 player. Your No.2 and No.3 players both sprint down the sidelines while looking for a quick pass if they are open. In this secondary break play, your No.1 should try to get the pass to either wing player (No.2 or No.3) as soon as possible, preferably to No.2 on the strong side. This is because if the defense does not get back in time, they may be able to go in towards the basket for a lay up. Your No.5 moves down to the strong side lo-post. Your No.4 moves to the top of the arc on the opposite side from your No.1. If your No.2 can see your No.5 breaking into the clear for a lay up, they pass them the ball. Otherwise they try to flash to the basket for a lay up, or jump shot.

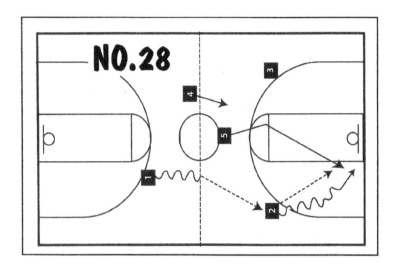

Motion No.2 Second Option No.29

If your No.2 has a defender between them and the basket, they pass the ball to your No.5. Your No.5 can then turn around and make a turnaround jump shot, or dribble the ball in for a lay up. Your No.2 then needs to follow their pass in, around back-door, for a possible rebound.

Motion No.3 Third Option   No.30

If your No.5 is not open, then your No.2 quickly passes the ball back out to your No.1. Then your No.1 quickly passes over to your No.4. While this is going on, your No.5 moves outside and sets a screen for No.2. Your No.2 immediately fakes going back-door to the basket, then cuts around the screen towards the middle of the lane, and looks for a pass. After screening out, Your No. 5 cuts back in towards the edge of the lane and tries to get clear for a pass.

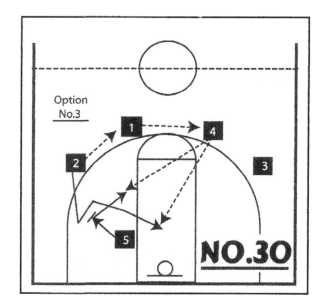

Motion No.4 Fourth Option   No.31

If the pass to your No.2 is not clear, then your No.4 holds the ball and waits for your No.2 to quickly move out to the 3 point arc for a shot. When your No.3 can see that your No.2 is moving out to the 3 point arc, they move in and screen out for them. At that point your No.4 passes the ball to your No.2, who can try for a 3 point shot.

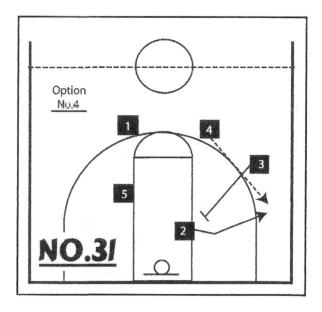

Motion No.5 Fifth Option   No.32

Just as your No.2 gets the pass from your No.4, Your No.5 player pulls their defender with them towards the free throw line elbow. Next your No.3 player sets a back screen for your No.5, who cuts back toward the basket off the screen. As they get close to the basket, your No.5 looks for a pass from your No.2, then they take it in for a lay up or a short jump shot.

Motion No.6 Sixth Option   No.33

If your No.5 player is covered and not in the clear for a pass, your No.2 can pass the ball back out to your No.4 player, to reload and set up a hi-lo series play. This is where your No.4 shoots a 3 point shot or a jumper. Or they pass it into your No.5 player on the lo- post, who hooks their defender and goes to the basket. As soon as your No.3 can see the ball is coming in to No.5, they quickly come across and screen for No.5.

Motion No.7 Seventh Option   No.34

If the hi-lo option is not open, then your No.2 holds the ball, and your No.3 moves out to the 3 point circle corner. Now you are reloaded to run "4 out- 1 in", Lo- post set plays.

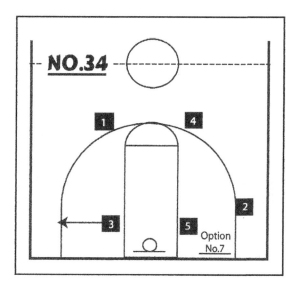

Motion No.8 Eight option   No.35

Or your No.2 can hold onto the ball while your No.1 moves over to the other side of the 3 point circle. Your No. 4 player screens for No.1, then moves down to the lo-post to block or screen for your No. 3 player. As soon as your No.4 player gets almost to the lo- post, your No.3 player moves out to the 3 point circle. Now you are reloaded to run "2 in - 3 out", set plays.

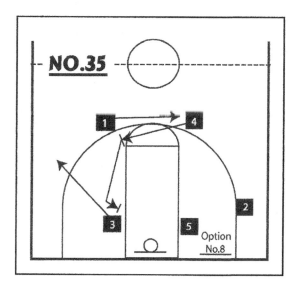

Working the Practice: Put all 5 to 10 players in position and run each secondary fast break play as shown on the diagram. Make sure to tell the defensive players to act out what they are supposed to do in their positions even though they know the play. The practice is for the offensive players so they must be at least partially clear to easily practice the play.

Emphasize; the players needing to make a fake and screen, where necessary, carry it out and, make it look good.

Run this Play: for about 30 minutes, then come back to it again another day. Getting as many run thru's as possible. If some players are not catching on to their part in the play, substitute, and have an assistant coach pull them aside and show them what they are doing wrong so that the practice does not stop and keeps going.

Out of Bounds Offensive Plays

Your "out of bounds" plays can be quick or slow, depending on what type of players you have, and what you want to do. Some coaches like to fast break off the out of bounds, and some don't. If you notice the defenders are not getting back on defense very quick, then you can probably run a fast break. If the defenders are getting back quickly, then it's probably best to slow it down and set up a play. Less chance of a turnover. Signal with your fingers or Yell" out what you want them to do.

Quick Out After a Score   (No.42)

Object of the play: Teach your players how to make a quick "Out of Bounds" play for a score.

What you will need: You will need about 2/3 of the court, a basketball, 5 offensive players, a couple of defenders if you need them, two coaches, and one whistle.

How the play works: This is a play to catch the opposition off guard. It can be run off a basket, a made free throw, or a rebound. For 12 year old and up teams, you can probably only run this play several times a game to fool them. Maybe you can save this play for near the end of the game when you really need a score badly. Your No.4 and No.5 players have to be around the basket or at the lo-post. This is basically a screen for your No.5, to get them down court quickly. Remember though you have to have a center that can run fast to make this play work. Right after the ball goes through the basket your No.4 player grabs the ball and takes it out quickly at the base line. Your No.5 sprints down across the court towards the left wing area. Your No.2 player moves over to screen the opposition's lo-post player, just long enough so that No.5 is free to sprint down court quickly. Your No.3 player moves back up to just over mid court then gets a long pass from your No.4 back at the base line. Then as your No.5 sprints by, they give them a little "give and go" type pass. Then No.3 turns and does a backside screen for any trailing opposition players. Your No.1 player runs down court, to fill the lane along the right side of the front court.

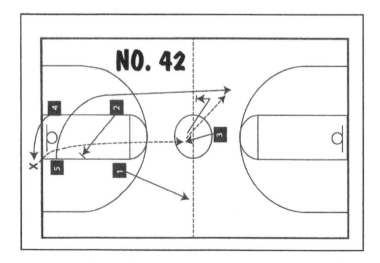

Working the Practice: Put all 10 players in position and run the play with No.3 getting the ball out by the center circle. Just for practice have the defenders not chase or cover No.3 so that they get practice on the play. Defenders just stay close and perform light pressure. With the young kids you may need to walk through this several time to make sure everyone knows their part.

Emphasize;   the No.3 player really getting the ball to No.5 then making a good back side screen for them. This allows No.5 to get clear on their way towards the basket.

Run this Play: for about 20 minutes. Getting as many run thru's as possible. If some players are not catching on to their part in the play, substitute and have an assistant coach pull them aside and show them what they are doing wrong so that the practice does not stop and keeps going

The Base Line Stack Play   (No.47)

Object of the play: Teach your players how to make the "Base Line Stack" play and beat the press to go down court or take a shot on their basket end.

What you will need: You will need about half of the court, a basketball, 5 offensive players, 3 defenders, two coaches, and one whistle.

How the play works;   This is the old "bread and butter" out of bounds play that I see almost all the youth teams using. Your No.1 takes the ball out at the base line. Your No.2, 3, 4, and 5, stack up along the edge of the lane. The variation I see some teams using is, they break in different directions off the basic stack. Your No.1 holds up one or two fingers, to designate which direction to go in.

On the basic stack, your No.2 is closest to the base line, then No.3 behind them, then No.4, and last No.5. Next your No.1 yells "BREAK". Then your No.5 breaks first towards the right elbow of the lane, then turns and reverses direction and goes to the top of the 3 point circle, next No.4 breaks to the left side 3 point circle. Your No.3 breaks next to the right lo post, and last your No. 2 breaks toward the left side 3 point circle. All the breaks should be in a quick sequence, one after the other. Have your players count by 1000's. No.1 looks to see who is most open, and passes them the ball. Your No.1 can then step right in to the left lo-post and fill the void left by No.2, or they break to the right side 3 point circle.

There can be all kinds of variations to the stack. I guess this is why so many teams use it, it's basic and pretty easy to teach. As an example, you can change the order of the players, from the base line out to the free throw line. Or you can change the direction each player breaks towards, to fool the defense. If you always break the same way each time, the defense will figure out how to defend against you. And maybe even get a steal or a turnover.

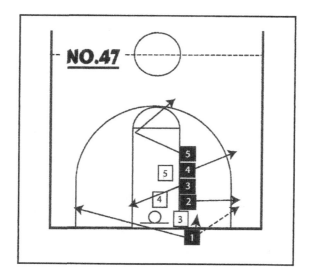

Working the practice: Have your players line up just like the diagram then scatter as indicated.

Emphasize: No.1 getting the ball out quickly to No.2 the first time as soon as they are open, then No.2 makes a pass to whoever is open for a shot. Passing from the base line to a different player each time so that the defense can't make a steal

Run this activity: for about only 20 minutes while making sure every player gets at least several chances to work on the play.

The Base Line Back Stack Play (No.48)

Object of the play: Teach your players how to make the "Base Line Back Stack" play and beat the press to go down court or take a shot on their basket end.

What you will need: You will need about half of the court, a basketball, 5 offensive players, 3 defenders, two coaches, and one whistle.

How the play works; This is a play that can work for the older kids, 12 years old and up. This can work especially if your team is having problems taking the ball out and getting it back in. This play works best against a zone defense. These stack plays should work with the breaks coming in quick, one after the other sequence. Have your players count by 1000's after they hear "BREAK", then break when their number comes up. Your No.1 takes the ball out at the base line. Then they yell "BREAK". Your No.4 moves first towards the basket, then sets a screen for your No.3 and No.5 players. They screen the defender in front of them, or the closest. Then No.4 holds the screen as long as they can. Your No.3 and No.5 players break together, do a "criss cross" around the screen, then head for the lo-post on each side. To make this work, your No.4 has to be a physically strong player. After your No.3 and No.5 players have cleared the screen, No.4 moves out to the 3 point circle. Your No.2 player is the safety valve option, they fake to their right, then move out to the left wing area. If they are open, your No.1 passes to No.3 or No.5 at the lo-post, as the main target for a shot at the basket. If they are not open, No.1 passes out to No.2, who holds the ball to set up a set play. After passing the ball, No.1 moves quickly under the basket, and around No.3, who blocks for them as they go by, to the right wing.

Working the practice: Have your players line up just like the diagram then scatter as indicated.

Emphasize: No.1 getting the ball out quickly to No.2 the first time as soon as they are open, then No.2 makes a pass to whoever is open for a shot. Passing from the base line to a different player each time so that the defense can't make a steal.

Run this activity: for about only 20 minutes while making sure every player gets at least several chances to work on the play.

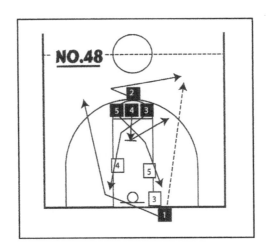

Breaking the Press Offensive Plays

Note: As you probably know, the rules will not let the little kids work the press, except in certain situations at the end of the game, and in the lower age groups. When they get older, teach them how beating the press works so that when it is used, they know how to break it.

The Side Line Press Breaker Play   (No.53, 54, 55)

Object of the play: Teach your players how to make the "Side Line Press Breaker" play and successfully get the ball inbounds when you are down near your offensive basket and the press is on. There are 3 motions to this play

What you will need: You will need the full court, a basketball, 5 offensive players, several defenders if you need them, two coaches, and one whistle.

For Motion No.1   No.53:   Your No.5 takes the ball out at the sideline. Your No.5 yells "BREAK" then your No.1 screens for your No.2, who breaks for the basket. If No.2 gets open, your No.5 passes them the ball. They either dribble it in for a lay up, or they stop and shoot a short jump shot. No.4 stays back at the other end of the court as a safety, in case there is a steal or a turnover.

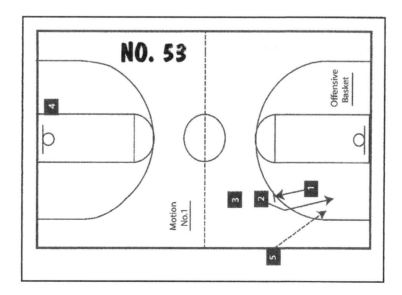

For Motion No.2   No.54:   There are several options here. When your No.1 can see that the pass is not going to No.2, they gets a screen from your No.3 player, reverse their direction, go

around, and break for the basket. The play then goes 2 on 1 to the basket. The problem with this play is going to be the 5 second rule. Your players will have to count by 1000's and move quickly so that your No.5 can inbound the ball in time.

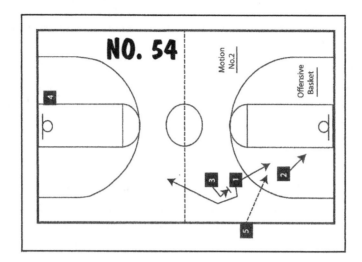

For Motion No.3 No.55: If your No.1 can see that there is no room to break for the basket, they go around the No.3 screen, and out towards the center court. Your No.5 then passes them the ball, and they reload the offense. And remember, the pass has to get out to your No.1 before the time runs out. If time is running short as they count, No. 1 has to get the pass as they run by No.5. Your No.2 breaks for the right wing area to decoy defenders into following them, and clearing the area around the basket.

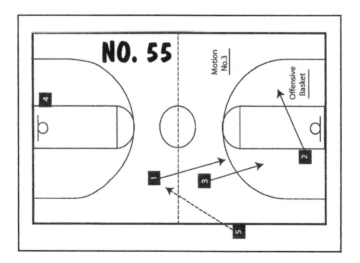

Working the practice: Have your players line up just like the diagram then run the play as indicated.

Emphasize: No.5 quickly getting the ball to the breaking No.2 if they are clear. or to No.3 back outside.

Run this activity: for about only 30 minutes while making sure every player gets at least several chances to work on the play.

Full Court Press Breaker Plays

Note: As you probably know, the rules will not let the little kids work the press, except in certain situations at the end of the game, and in the older age groups. When they get older, teach them how beating the press works so that when it is used, they know how to break it. Some simple rules, and strategy, for beating the full court press. ***Stay calm***, think what you are doing. ***Attack***, be positive and attack the pressure. ***Use 3 Looks***, look up the court and not down at the ball, look before you pass, look before you dribble, don't dribble unless you have to, sharp quick passes beat the press not dribbling. ***Avoid trap areas*** (see the diagram), keep away from these areas. ***Getting the ball inbounds***, inbound the ball quickly before the defense can set up. ***Quick accurate passing***, find the open man and make quick accurate passes. ***Receivers meet the pass***, go to the ball and get open. ***Use the whole court***, reverse the ball to the opposite side if you have to. ***Have a standard press break play***, one that works for you, then yell "PRESS BREAK" to them when you see it coming.

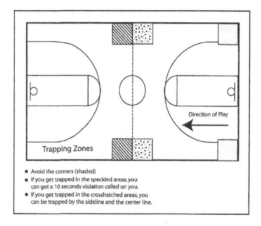

Beating the 1-2-1-1 Full Court Press (No.56, 57)

Note; The weakness of the 1-2-1-1 is up the sideline, or at mid court. Have one of your post players (No. 4 or No.5) inbound the ball as quickly as possible. You will have to practice this so that everyone knows their positions, and goes to them quickly before the press can set up.

Object of the play: Teach your players how to beat the "1-2-1-1 Full Court Press" and successfully get the ball inbounds when you are down near your defensive basket and the press is on. There are 2 motions to this play

What you will need: You will need the full court, a basketball, 5 offensive players, 5 defenders, two coaches, and one whistle.

For Motion No.1 No.56: Your No.4 player takes the ball out at the base line. Next they yell "BREAK", and your primary target No.1 comes back down towards the ball on the right side of the court. If they are open they get the inbounds pass. Your No.2 player breaks down towards the basket in the lane, and looks for a pass if they are open and No.1 is not. If the pass goes over to No.1, then No.2 reverses and breaks back up the court on the left sideline. At the same time your No.3 player breaks to the top of the key, and No.5 breaks to the right wing area. After the pass is made, your No.4 player moves across and up the lane the lane, from under the basket.

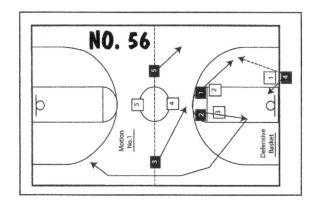

For Motion No.2   No.57:   Once the ball has been inbounded, and your No.1 has the ball, they quickly pass to your No.5, No.3, or No.4. With No.5 being the primary target, and next No.3, and your No.4 last as a safety. If No.5 gets the pass the rest of the team goes immediately into a fast break set play down the court. If your No. 3 gets the pass, they immediately pass to your No.2 who has stopped over on the left sideline near center court. If your No.4 player gets the pass they immediately pass to either No.2 or No.3, with No.2 being the primary target. Once the ball is basically out of the back court, they can go into secondary fast break set play.

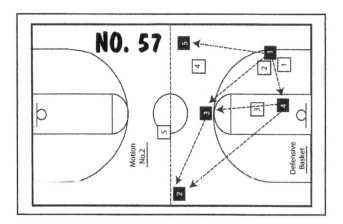

Working the practice: Have your players line up just like the diagram then run the play as indicated.

Emphasize: No.4 getting the pass over to No.2 if they are clear or to No.1 breaking into the flat.

Run this activity: for about only 30 minutes while making sure every player gets at least several chances to work on the play.

Simplified 4 Across Press Breaker (No.63, 64)

Note; This is a little different player positioning that I think makes it a little easier for the little kids to understand. A little less movement, and quicker too.

Object of the play: Teach your younger players a simplified way to beat the " Full Court Press" and successfully get the ball inbounds when you are down near your defensive basket and the press is on. There are 2 motions to this play

What you will need: You will need the full court, a basketball, 5 offensive players, several defenders if you need them, two coaches, and one whistle.

For Motion No.1   No.63:   Your No.5 player takes the ball out at the base line. Your No.1 and No.2 line up on the inside on this one. No.5 yells "BREAK", and instead of a double screen, your No.2 sets a screen for your No.1. Your No.1 then moves around in back of the screen, and gets the inbounds pass from No.5. At the same time your No.3 and No.4 players both fake a move towards No.5, like they are going to get the pass, then both turn around and break back up court in the sideline lanes. Your No.2 moves to the left side corner after screening, to act as a safety valve for the inbounds pass.

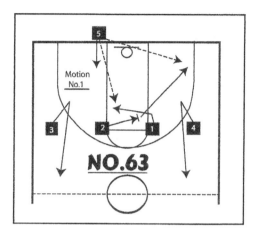

For Motion No.2   No.64:   Your No.1 gets the inbounds pass, dribbles a few feet up court, then looks to pass to either your No.3 or No.4 players cutting down the court. If the defenders collapse on your No.1, then No.5 passes to your No.2 in the corner. Then they start to dribble up the court, and look for your No.3 or No.4 players to pass to. Whoever gets the pass can then go into a secondary fast break set play up the court. No.5 is the "trailer" on the fast break.

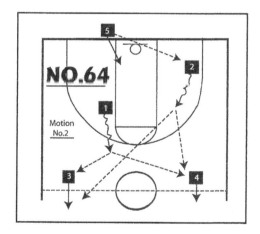

Working the practice: Have your players line up just like the diagram then run the play as indicated.

Emphasize: No.5 getting the pass over to No.1 while the other players make their fakes.

Run this activity: for about only 30 minutes while making sure every player gets at least several chances to work on the play.

Delay Offensive Plays

Note: Sometimes you need a delay play when you need to take time off the clock, like maybe near the end of the game when you are ahead in the score. Here is a good play to use. Also if you have the lead and the opponent changes to a zone defense, the counter strategy is go to the spread, make them go into a man to man and come out at you. However if the defenders do come way out after you, and your No.1 (your key player in the middle) or any of the other players can see an uncontested easy lay up, tell them to take it. Coaches sometimes call these plays "butter with a spread", or just "butter", or "soft butter".

4 Corners Spread Play (No.65 to 69)

Note; The way it is set up, there are some "RULES" for each of your players to follow: There are 5 motion options to this play.

Object of the play: Teach your younger players how to run the '4 Corners' spread play to run minutes off the clock when you need a delay.

What you will need: You will need half the court, a basketball, 5 offensive players, several defenders if you need them, two coaches, and one whistle.

No.1 Chaser Point Guard Motion No.1 No.65:
1. When dribbling, pass before a double team collapses on them.
2. After passing, cut and quickly get open to receive the pass back to them.
3. If they can't get the pass back, cut to the basket, or replace either No.2 or No.3 in the corner.

Wing Players (No.2 and No.3) Motion No.1 No.65:
1. Make sure they stay in the corners, about 6 feet from half court line and the sideline.
2. If not pressured after receiving a pass, hold the ball until the defense comes out to them, then pass the ball back to No.1.
3. If the defense is blocking No.1 from getting the pass back, dribble the ball to center court and become the new chaser (No.1). The old chaser moves to the vacated corner where NO. 3 was.

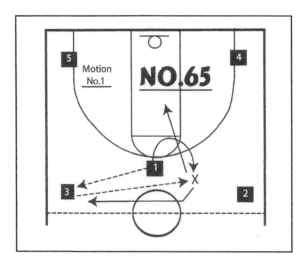

For Post Players (No.4 and No.5) Motion No.2   No.66:
1. If the pass goes to the opposite corner, the weak side player No.5 cuts to the low post on the ball side, for a block or screen **(No.66)**.

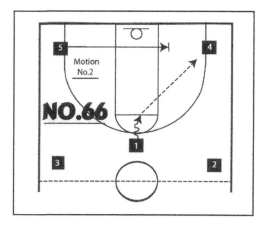

2. If the post players defender moves over to trap the chaser (No.1), then No.5 quickly cuts to the basket for a pass from No.1. Then goes for the lay up **(No.67)**.

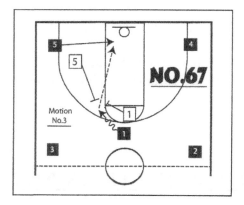

3. If the chaser or a wing player is in trouble, or they stop their dribble, cut up the sideline to a spot in line with the free throw line extended, and look to receive a pass **(No.68)**.

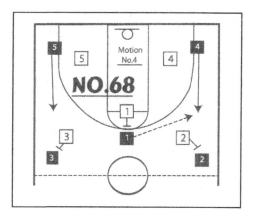

4. If the post player guarding them over plays them, and keeps them from receiving the pass, then they cut back quickly to the basket for a pass from No.1 **(No.69)**.

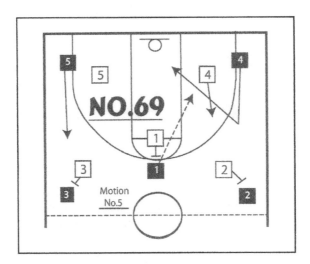

Working the practice: Have your players line up just like the diagrams then run the play as indicated.

Emphasize: No.1 making the right decisions depending on what's happening.

Run this activity: for about only 30 minutes while making sure every player gets at least several chances to work on the play.

12. OFFENSIVE TRAINING GAMES

Note: All offensive training games will be numbered for "EASY " reference.

These are games you can have your team play once in a while. This will break up the practice from endless drills. The kids are learning a skill, but having a little fun at the same time.

Skill Activity No. 155- *The Bean Bag Game*

The Object of the game is: Players learn how to dribble without stopping, just like in a real game.

The Basics of the game are:

This game will help your players develop good dribbling skills. Split up into three teams. On the whistle one player from each team dribbles towards the pile of 12 bean bags near the top of the key. Without stopping their dribble they reach down and grab just one bean bag. They dribble back to their team and deposit the bean bag. Then they give the basketball to the next player on their team. That player does the same thing until all the bean bags in the pile are gone. After that they can dribble over and steal the other teams bean bags until the whistle blows to end the game. This keeps going on until all the bean bags in the circle are gone. Waiting players can not stop them from stealing. After two minutes of play the team with the most bean bags wins. This is a half court game.

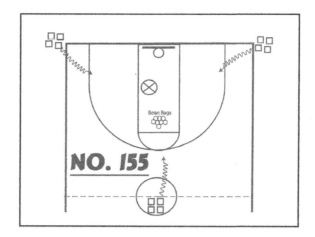

What you will need to play the game:
You will need 3 basketballs, 12 bean bags, 3 teams of players, 2 coaches, and a whistle.

How to play the game:
Here is how it works. Put one team at center court. The other two teams go to the two corners of the base line. Each team has one ball. Place twelve bean bags in a pile in the key circle. On your whistle one player from each team dribbles into the key circle, then while still dribbling each player reaches down and picks up a bean bag. They need to keep the dribble going at all times. Next they dribble back to their team and while still dribbling they deposit the bean bag in a pile right at center court or at the corner lines. The RULE is they can only take one bean bag at a time. Waiting players can not interfere with players that are active, like keeping them from stealing a bean bag.

How long to play the game:
The game runs for 2 minutes than coach blows the whistle ending the game.

How to make the game easier or harder:
If the game is to hard for the younger kids then bring the starting points in closer, mark the spot with cones.

If the game is to easy for the older kids then add more bean bags. Then if they stop their dribble at any point make them go halfway back to the starting point from that spot and start their dribble over.

Skill Activity No. 157- *The Obstacle Course Relay Game*

The Object of the game is: Players develop their skill of dribbling around opponent's, just like in a real game.

The Basics of the game are:
This game will help your players develop good speed and defensive dribbling skills. The game is split into two teams. Half of a team is on one side of the court, and half on the other side. This is a relay race. On your whistle the front player on both teams starts weave dribbling around each cone to the other side line. When they have passed the side line (A RULE) they hand off to their team mate on that side. The team mate dribbles back through the course and hands off to the next team mate. This can go on for ten minutes. Whichever team is ahead at that point wins the game.

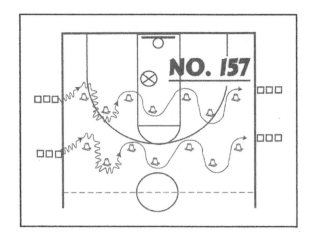

What you will need to play the game:
You will need 2 basketballs, 14 Orange cones, 2 teams of players, 2 coaches, and a whistle.
How to play the game:
Here is how it works. Split each team in half, half on one side of the court, half on the other side. On your whistle the front player on each team starts dribbling across the court around the cones. When they get to the other side they hand the basketball off to the next player in line. That player dribbles across and hands of. This keeps going on until coach blows the whistle to end the game. The RULE is they need to pass the side line before they can hand off. No cheating and passing ahead to a teammate. If they loose the ball they go halfway back to the starting point from that spot and start dribbling over again from there.
How long to play the game:
The game runs for 10 minutes than coach blows the whistle ending the game.
How to make the game easier or harder:
If the game is to hard for the younger kids then eliminate half the cones, and bring the starting points in closer, mark the spot with cones.

Skill Activity No. 158- *The "HORSE" Game*
The Object of the game is: Players develop their skill for making baskets, just like in a real game.
The Basics of the game are:
This game will help your players with their shooting accuracy. You can adapt it for your team. Line up all your players at the half court line. You will probably need a note book to keep track of the letters each player has. The first player tries to make a shot, any kind they like. Then they go to the end of the line. If the second player makes the exact same shot then they go to the end of the line. If they miss the shot they get a letter "H." After a miss the next player in line gets to pick their shot. It keeps going until there is a miss. That player gets the next letter until the word "H-O-R-S-E" is spelled out. When a player gets all the letters then they are out of the game. The last player left without all the letters wins the game.

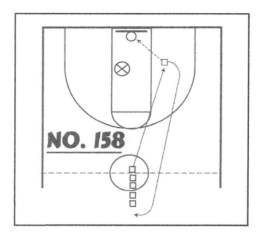

What you will need to play the game:
You will need 1 basketball, a pencil and notebook to keep score, 2 coaches, and a whistle.

How to play the game:
Here is how it works. Line everyone up at center court. Have the first player in the line move up and take any shot they like until they make the basket, then they go to the end of the line. The next player in line has ONE chance to go out and make the same exact shot from the same place. If they make it they go to the end of the line. If they miss the shot they get an "H" after their name. Then the next player in line goes out and gets to pick any shot they like until they make it. Then the next player comes up and has to make the same exact shot. If they make it they go to the end of the line. If they miss they get an "H" after their name. After the player gets their next miss they get an "O" after their name. This keeps going on until they have "H-O-R-S-E" spelled out after their name. Then they are out of the game. The last player left without "HORSE" completely spelled out after their name wins the game. One coach keeps track of the letters after each players name.

How long to play the game:
The game runs for 1 hour or until there is a winner, then coach blows the whistle ending the game. This game can run for a long time with the older kids. If time runs out in practice what you can do is keep track of the score the pick up where it left off on the next time you play the game. OR you can just call the player with the fewest letters the winner.

Skill Activity No. 159- *The "Around the World" Game*

The Object of the game is: Players develop their skill for making baskets from different part of the court.

The Basics of the game are:
This is a game to help your players with their shot accuracy and their shot distance. Each spot for a shot is marked. From "A" to "T." Split the team up into groups of three. The first player on one team starts at the letter "A." Players get 2 shot attempts at each letter. If the make the shot they go to the next letter when it's their turn again. If they miss the first shot they have options for the second shot. If they defer to shoot it moves to the first player on the next team. Player need to make shots all the way around to the letter "T." The first team with a player to get all the way around to the letter "T" and make it wins the game.

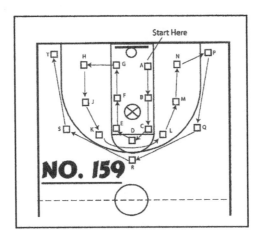

What you will need to play the game:

You will need 1 basketball, a pencil and notebook to keep track of where the teams are, Some tape or cones to mark the shot spots, 2 coaches, and a whistle.

How to play the game:

Here is how it works. The first player on one of the teams starts at the letter "A." Players get 2 shot attempts at each letter. If the make the shot they go to the next letter when it's their turn again. Then it goes to the next player on the next team. They shoot until they miss then it moves to the next team (they take turns). Remember they are given 2 attempts to make the shot. If they miss the first shot they have options for the second shot. If a player misses their first attempt, they can elect to stop at that spot then give the ball to the next shooter on the following team. Then they start at that spot when it is their next turn. If they elect to shoot the second shot and miss it, they give the ball up to the next shooter and go to the end of their line. On their next turn they go back and start over at spot where they missed and try again. If they defer to shoot their second shot it moves to the first player on the next team. This keeps going on until one team gets to "T" and makes the shot. Someone on a team needs to make the shots all the way around to the letter "T" in order for that team to win

How long to play the game:

The game runs for 1 hour or until there is a winner, then coach blows the whistle ending the game. This game can run for a long time with the younger kids. If time runs out in practice what you can do is keep track of which team is where, then pick up where it left off on the next time you play the game. OR you can just call the team that gets to the fewest letters the winner.

How to make the game easier or harder:

If the game is to hard for the younger kids here is what you can do. Move all the spots in closer. If the game is to easy for the older kids here is what you can do. There are variations. After going all the way to the top letter ("T"), have players return in reverse order. Have players use their right arm, then the left, on every other shot Have players use only their weak arm (left). Or the backboard must always be used to bank in a shot.

13. TYPICAL PRACTICE SCHEDULES

Why Have Practice Schedules

When you lay out a practice schedule, kids learn more, and faster (Practice is usually 1 hour for beginners). You can't always follow it to the letter, but you try to follow it as close as possible within reason. I know many of you coaches don't like to follow a schedule, but if you do, you are going to find that the kids learn a lot more, do it quicker, and their skills improve much faster. The secret is plan out what you want to teach each session, the get some assistant coaches to help, as many as possible. They can even be parents, who may just be sitting around doing nothing watching anyway, might as well put them to work. It's not hard if you just show them EXACTLY what it is you want them to do. I do this all the time. And I find that many parents are willing to help as long as you show them EXACTLY what it is you want them to do. We will put some different types of 1 hour sample schedules together for you to see some different ways how to do it. This is because most young teams are only given 1 hour in the gym. If you have more than an hour to practice then just add the next schedule to it. The idea is to show you how to teach larger groups the same fundamentals in 2 days instead of 3 or 4.

1 Hour Sample Schedules

METHOD 1- BEGINNERS
(Smaller Groups of up to 9)
Practice 1 (One Coach, One Asst.)

Coach Plus Asst. (Whole Group)
4:00 to 4:10 Stretching and Exercising (All Together)
4:10 to 4:20 Holding the Ball Drill
4:20 to 4:25 Water Break
4:25 to 4:35 Proper Shooting Stance Drill
4:35 to 4:45 Proper Shooting Mechanics Drill
4:45 to 4:50 Water Break
4:50 to 5:00 Sit on the Chair Training Drill
5:00 to 5:05 End of Practice Closure (All Together)

Practice 2 (One Coach, One Asst.)

Coach Plus Asst. (Whole Group)
4:00 to 4:10 Stretching and Exercising (All Together)
4:10 to 4:20 Proper Body Mechanics Training Drill
4:20 to 4:25 Water Break
4:25 to 4:35 Bank Shot Shooting Drill
4:35 to 4:45 Lay On the Floor Training Drill
4:45 to 4:50 Water Break
4:50 to 5:00 Around the Chair Screen Drill
5:00 to 5:05 End of Practice Closure (All Together)

METHOD 2- BEGINNERS
(For Large Groups of 10 to 20)
Practice 1 (One Coach, One Assistant)

Note: Split into Two Groups
4:00 to 4:10 Stretching and Exercising (All Together)
Coach- Group 1
4:10 to 4:20 Release and Follow Through Drill
4:20 to 4:25 Water Break
4:25 to 4:35 Lay Up Shot Training Drill
4:35 to 4:45 Set Shot Jumper Training Drill
4:45 to 4:50 Water Break
4:50 to 5:00 Hook Shot Training Drill
5:00 to 5:05 End of Practice Closure (All Together)

Assistant- Group 2 (Simultaneously)
4:10 to 4:20 Basic dribbling Training Drill
4:20 to 4:25 Water Break
4:25 to 4:35 Either Hand Dribbling Training Drill
4:35 to 4:45 No Look Dribble Training Drill
4:45 to 4:50 Water Break
4:50 to 5:00 Controlled Half Court Dribbling Drill
5:00 to 5:05 End of Practice Closure (All Together)

Practice 2 (One Coach, One Assistant)

Note: Still Split into Two Groups
4:00 to 4:10 Stretching and Exercising (All Together)
Coach- Group 2
4:10 to 4:20 Two Hands Chest Pass Training Drill
4:20 to 4:25 Water Break
4:25 to 4:35 Both Hands Bounce Pass Training Drill
4:35 to 4:45 Two Hand Overhead Pass Training Drill
4:45 to 4:50 Water Break
4:50 to 5:00 One Hand Pass Training Drill
5:00 to 5:05 End of Practice Closure (All Together)

Assistant- Group 1 (Simultaneously)
4:10 to 4:20 High Speed Dribbling Drill
4:20 to 4:25 Water Break
4:25 to 4:35 Hesitate/Stutter Step Dribbling Drill
4:35 to 4:45 Behind the Back Dribbling Drill
4:45 to 4:50 Water Break
4:50 to 5:00 Switch Hands Crossover Dribbling Drill
5:00 to 5:05 End of Practice Closure (All Together)

METHOD 3- BEGINNERS
(For Large Groups of 10 to 20)

Practice 1 (One Coach, One Assistant)

Note: Split into Two Groups
4:00 to 4:10 Stretching and Exercising (All Together)
Coach- Group 1
4:10 to 4:20 Through The Legs Dribbling Drill
4:20 to 4:25 Water Break
4:25 to 5:00 The "HORSE" Shooting Game on One End of the Court
5:00 to 5:05 End of Practice Closure (All Together)

Assistant- Group 2 (Simultaneously)
4:10 to 4:20 Spin Move Dribbling Drill
4:20 to 4:25 Water Break
4:25 to 5:00 The "HORSE" Shooting Game on the Other End of the Court
5:00 to 5:05 End of Practice Closure (All Together)

Practice 2 (One Coach, One Assistant)

Note: Split into Two Groups
4:00 to 4:10 Stretching and Exercising (All Together)
Coach- Group 1
4:10 to 4:20 Shuffle Dribbling Drill
4:20 to 4:25 Water Break
4:25 to 5;00 The Bean Bag Game (All Together)
5:00 to 5:05 End of Practice Closure (All Together)

Assistant- Group 2 (Simultaneously)
4:10 to 4:20 Change of Pace Dribbling Drill
4:20 to 4:25 Water Break
4:25 to 5;00 The Bean Bag Game (All Together)
5:00 to 5:05 End of Practice Closure (All Together)

METHOD 4- BEGINNERS
(For Large Groups of up to 20)

Practice 1 (Multiple Coaches- Stations- Groups Rotate From 1-2-3)

Note: Split into Three Groups
4:00 to 4:10 Stretching and Exercising (All Together)
Head Coach- Group 1
4:10 to 4:20 Holding the Ball Drill

4:20 to 4:25 Water Break
4:25 to 4:35 Proper Shooting Stance Drill
4:35 to 4:45 Proper Shooting Mechanics Drill
4:45 to 4:50 Water Break
4:50 to 5:00 Lay on the Floor Training Drill
5:00 to 5:05 End of Practice Closure (All Together)

Assistant- Group 2 (Simultaneously)
4:10 to 4:20 Two Hands Chest Pass Drill
4:20 to 4:25 Water Break
4:25 to 4:35 Both Hands Bounce Pass Training Drill
4:35 to 4:45 Two Hands Overhead pass Training Drill
4:45 to 4:50 Water Break
4:50 to 5:00 One Hand Pass Training Drill
5:00 to 5:05 End of Practice Closure (All Together)

Assistant- Group 3 (Simultaneously)
4:10 to 4:20 High Speed Dribbling Drill
4:20 to 4:25 Water Break
4:25 to 4:35 Hesitate/Stutter Step Dribbling Drill
4:35 to 4:45 Behind the Back Dribbling Drill
4:45 to 4:50 Water Break
4:50 to 5:00 Switch Hands Crossover Dribbling Drill
5:00 to 5:05 End of Practice Closure (All Together)

Practice 2 (Multiple Coaches- Stations- Groups Rotate From 1-2-3)

Note: Split into Three Groups
4:00 to 4:10 Stretching and Exercising (All Together)
Head Coach- Group 3
4:10 to 4:20 Holding the Ball Drill
4:20 to 4:25 Water Break
4:25 to 4:35 Proper Shooting Stance Drill
4:35 to 4:45 Proper Shooting Mechanics Drill
4:45 to 4:50 Water Break
4:50 to 5:00 Lay on the Floor Training Drill
5:00 to 5:05 End of Practice Closure (All Together)

Assistant- Group 1 (Simultaneously)
4:10 to 4:20 Two Hands Chest Pass Drill
4:20 to 4:25 Water Break
4:25 to 4:35 Both Hands Bounce Pass Training Drill
4:35 to 4:45 Two Hands Overhead pass Training Drill
4:45 to 4:50 Water Break
4:50 to 5:00 One Hand Pass Training Drill
5:00 to 5:05 End of Practice Closure (All Together)

Assistant- Group 2 (Simultaneously)
4:10 to 4:20 High Speed Dribbling Drill
4:20 to 4:25 Water Break
4:25 to 4:35 Hesitate/Stutter Step Dribbling Drill
4:35 to 4:45 Behind the Back Dribbling Drill
4:45 to 4:50 Water Break
4:50 to 5:00 Switch Hands Crossover Dribbling Drill
5:00 to 5:05 End of Practice Closure (All Together)

Practice 3 (Multiple Coaches- Stations- Groups Rotate From 1-2-3)

Note: Split into Three Groups
4:00 to 4:10 Stretching and Exercising (All Together)
Head Coach- Group 2
4:10 to 4:20 Holding the Ball Drill
4:20 to 4:25 Water Break
4:25 to 4:35 Proper Shooting Stance Drill

4:35 to 4:45 Proper Shooting Mechanics Drill
4:45 to 4:50 Water Break
4:50 to 5:00 Lay on the Floor Training Drill
5:00 to 5:05 End of Practice Closure (All Together)

Assistant- Group 3 (Simultaneously)
4:10 to 4:20 Two Hands Chest Pass Drill
4:20 to 4:25 Water Break
4:25 to 4:35 Both Hands Bounce Pass Training Drill
4:35 to 4:45 Two Hands Overhead pass Training Drill
4:45 to 4:50 Water Break
4:50 to 5:00 One Hand Pass Training Drill
5:00 to 5:05 End of Practice Closure (All Together)

Assistant- Group 1 (Simultaneously)
4:10 to 4:20 High Speed Dribbling Drill
4:20 to 4:25 Water Break
4:25 to 4:35 Hesitate/Stutter Step Dribbling Drill
4:35 to 4:45 Behind the Back Dribbling Drill
4:45 to 4:50 Water Break
4:50 to 5:00 Switch Hands Crossover Dribbling Drill
5:00 to 5:05 End of Practice Closure (All Together)

Scheduling Summation

There are all kinds of ways to set up training. And they may all work, but some ways are better than others because they are more efficient. Also progression is probably a better way to go. In other words start with what fundamental skill they need to know first before they start the next one. Also it may be a good idea to have the coach one day, and the assistant the next day, teaching the same skill. It's like batting in baseball, some kids will catch on with one particular technique over another, and be successful with it. Such as how they swing the bat or how they pitch. So maybe another coaches technique will help a young beginner learn how to do something in another way that will make them successful.

Note:

In 3 days or practices up to 20 kids may have been taught all the above different fundamental techniques shown.

What is "**End of Practice Closure**?" You have all your kids come together then go quickly over how the days practice went. Tell them they did an awesome job. Give them any reminders or notices. Then all the players get in a big circle together with a hand up in the middle all touching. Then coach says, "One two three" and everyone yells "Yeah Team" or whatever they want to yell. This way kids all go home on a good note.

THE END

June 2014

CPSIA information can be obtained at www.ICGtesting.com
Printed in the USA
LVOW02s0637111113

360802LV00001B/3/P